4 a

D0919620

THE FRENCH ECONOMY 1913-39

By the same author

INDUSTRIALIZATION IN NINETEENTH
CENTURY EUROPE (Longman)

THEORIES OF IMPERIALISM (Dobson)

ECONOMIC FORCES IN FRENCH HISTORY (Dobson)

TOM KEMP

THE FRENCH ECONOMY 1913-39 The history of a decline

LONGMAN

LONGMAN GROUP LIMITED
London

Associated companies, branches and
representatives throughout the world

© Longman Group Limited 1972

First published 1972

ISBN 0 582 48248 8

Printed in Great Britain by
Hazell Watson & Viney Ltd,
Aylesbury, Bucks.

CONTENTS

PREFACE

The purpose of this study is to provide an interpretative account of French economic history from just before the First World War to the eve of the Second. In the main this was a period of retrogression and decline expressing a deep-seated crisis in bourgeois society the symptoms of which, by the 1930s, had become patently obvious. While this crisis had economic roots it cannot be explained purely in economic terms and this book does not profess to provide a full and rounded account—which would require an examination of the political developments and the social and cultural trauma of the period. It remains, therefore, the contribution of an economic historian to the problem of France's decline and collapse in 1940 which will have to be complemented and completed, even if its major thesis is accepted, by studies which begin from a different standpoint.

It is no accident that the writing of this work was influenced by the events of May–June 1968 and their aftermath which showed that, despite the boom in which France had shared during the 1960s, the long-term crisis in French society, which had first revealed itself in the interwar period, remained unresolved. Nevertheless, although much of what follows was written within a short space of time in the summer of 1970, the origin of the book goes back to a summer twenty-six years before when, as an obscure member of the invading forces, the author landed on the shores of southern France. Then more than now, this was an area which bore all the signs of economic retardation and under-development. The contact set going a train of enquiry into the reasons for this.

Closer and more intimate acquaintance with French life confirmed the impression that, in many ways, France had not advanced into the twentieth century, or only in a one-sided way. The developments since then have aggravated tensions and contradictions despite the steady and at times spectacular rates of economic growth which have been achieved. Undoubtedly since 1945 French society has experienced great changes, but the weight of history cannot be easily thrown off; the problems posed in the 1930s by the confrontation between the working-class and bourgeois society exploded once again in 1968 and not for the last time.

Over the past quarter of a century I have had many and varied contacts with French people in many walks of life, of different levels of education and of diverse political opinions. Through discussion, observation and participation these contacts have no doubt contributed to the views expressed in this book. Apart from that, I have no obligations to record and my responsibility for its shortcomings are all the greater. However, I am grateful to the Houblon-Norman Fund which made a grant in 1969–70 enabling me to consult material only accessible in French libraries.

To my French parents-in-law I am indebted in many ways. To their son René, a great pilot whose loss in a banal accident was a blow to French aviation, I really owe my deeper acquaintance with his country without which this book would probably not have been written.

It is a tribute to my own neglectfulness that my wife and family were unaware that this book was being written.

My thanks are due to my wife and to my colleague Mike Brown for their help with the tedious task of proof-reading.

T.K.

Department of Economic and Social History
The University, Hull

I

INTRODUCTION

In the history of modern France economic forces do not receive the attention they deserve. There is a paucity of economic texts in English and even in French: Clapham and Sée still do service despite the considerable volume of monographic work done since their books appeared.[1] The more recent period has suffered still more seriously from neglect. Until the appearance of Alfred Sauvy's volumes there was no economic history of the interwar period.[2] While the present work has made use of this study, as every student in the field must, it approaches the problems of the period from a different point of view and from one which is more strictly that of the economic historian. Professor Sauvy, who was a contemporary of the events he describes and played some part in them towards the close, is mainly concerned with questions of public policy, losing no opportunity to comment with acerbity on the failings and

1. J. H. Clapham, *The Economic Development of France and Germany,* (4th edition, 1936); H. Sée, *Histoire économique de la France, II, Les Temps Modernes,* Paris, 1951. See also S. B. Clough, *France: a history of national economics,* reprint, 1964 and T. Kemp, *Economic Forces in French History* (London, 1971).
2. A. Sauvy, *Histoire économique de la France entre les deux guerres,* 2 vols., Paris, 1965, 1967.

foibles of his countrymen. Both from the standpoint of analysing the structure of the French economy and in his discussion of the problems of development his work, for all its value as a guide, leaves the reader unsatisfied. There is, however, no pretension here to fill these gaps and it would, in any case, be presumptuous as well as premature to do so in view of the lack of basic studies of many aspects of development.

The catalogue of what is missing from the literature is impressive. Of what went on in the large industrial, banking and commercial firms we know little or nothing. Histories of particular industries are scarce. Studies of particular problems and periods in twentieth-century French economic history are few. The relations between business and government are largely a matter for conjecture. Economic policy-making at the government level is likewise shrouded in mystery. What influence the 'two hundred families' of legend exercised has never been determined.[3] What constituted the *mur d'argent* has never been made clear. There has been no lack of assertions or of theorising of a general sort, but solid studies, either empirical or theoretical scarcely exist. The political history of modern France has appeared intrinsically more absorbing, and, of course, it is better documented. The nature of official statistics even in the 'thirties makes it difficult to apply sophisticated types of analysis. Perhaps Frenchmen prefer to forget the dismal economic record of the 'thirties.

A single book cannot hope to fill all these gaps and it should be pointed out to begin with what it does not set out to do. It is not a factual history derived from a study of documents and records describing the externals of economic life: production, trade, imports and exports, population and the like. The empirical material is used mainly to trace out and attempt to explain the main characteristics of development. What were the special forces which contributed to the physiognomy of French capitalism and how did it respond to the great crises of the period: the First World War, the world economic depression and the social and

3. The beginning of an attempt to study empirically the world of banking and finance and its connections with industry and politics was made by the translator of Bernard Shaw's works into French, Augustin Hamon, in *Les Maîtres de la France,* vols i–iii, 1936–38.

political crisis which heralded the onset of a new war? These are broadly the questions with which it is concerned. It does not claim to be an economic history of France, but rather to consider some aspects of that history, notably the critical turning points and the characteristic longer-term problems.

The period chosen for study is not difficult to justify. By beginning with a profile of the economy in 1913 it is possible to sum up the results of nineteenth-century development and to provide a picture of the economic scene at the end of a period of prosperity, stability and economic growth which became known as *la belle époque*. It was by no means *belle* for the majority of French people: for the peasant condemned to a life of endless toil and living under primitive sanitary and housing conditions; for the worker whose hours remained long, whose rights were still narrowly defined, who enjoyed little in the way of social security benefits and whose standard of living, although better than in the nineteenth century, still compared unfavourably with that of workers in other capitalist countries. Nevertheless, for capitalism this was a period of prosperity and progress, of monetary stability and safe profits. But French capitalism inherited from its past some special characteristics which held back the extent of industralisation and thus the *per capita* income and the immediate possibilities for more rapid growth without further structural change. These peculiarities have therefore to be examined and explained; we need to know something about the long-term trends before the effects of the First World War can be estimated.

On the eve of the war France was still pre-eminently a country of liberal capitalism in which the virtues of the free market were scarcely questioned and in which the economic activities of the state still remained minimal. Monopoly had made only small inroads into the competitive market structure, though more than many people realised. At the same time, it was characteristic that the economy preserved many archaic features bound up with the existence of a large agrarian sector largely dominated by the peasantry. This fact, together with certain archaisms in industrial production, suggests that although France was indubitably a country of advanced industrial capitalism its social and economic structures contained many features which were not fully congruous with its demands. Out of this contradiction arose conflicts and social strains which were to dominate the future history of the country.

The First World War was a tremendous traumatic experience in the lives of all classes; it marked a turning point in social and economic history. It made deep inroads into the male population of a country which was already suffering from a kind of demographic anaemia. It tore up many of the old landmarks by which the bourgeoisie had charted its course. It destroyed capital values which had been regarded as eternal. It ended currency stability which had lasted for over a century. It embittered the peasantry and turned it into a discontented force. It increased the specific weight of the proletariat and raised the spectre of social revolution. France's international role was much diminished. Never had a victor country won a war at such a high price in blood and treasure. The war had required the piecemeal establishment of economic controls, bringing the government into the economic arena on an unprecedented scale. The shibboleths about individual enterprise and the free market to which the bourgeoisie had been dedicated since the Revolution were reluctantly held in abeyance.

But that is all they were. One of the fruits of victory seemed obviously to be the early restoration of the free market. Controls were deliberately and swiftly abandoned as soon as something like normal conditions were restored. In other ways, however, the war had left an indelible mark. There was the heavy loss of life and all that meant in demographic terms for France, a country of only sons. There were the heavy financial burdens that the war left: interallied debts, and the heavy internal debt contracted to finance the war and reconstruction. It was expected that Germany would pay or, later, that the Allies would lighten the load. Neither happened; confidence in money was undermined and inflation was rampant. On the other hand the war appeared to have some positive and even invigorating effects. With Alsace-Lorraine France recovered three of her most highly industrialised and progressive departments,[4]

4. Part of Lorraine, the departments of Meurthe-et-Moselle and Meuse, remained French after the Treaty of Frankfort which annexed Alsace-Lorraine to Germany.

complete with the social security and other laws instituted by the Germans. But the war and reconstruction accelerated the pace of industrialisation in both old and new industrial regions. During the war industries had to be established in new areas far from the battle zone. The reconstructed northern and eastern departments, the main cradles of French industrialisation, were re-equipped in infrastructure and in productive forces largely at government expense. New branches of industry began to take root expressing the advanced technologies of the scientific age.

France was thus launched into a period of postwar prosperity and expansion which seemed to continue the growth of the pre-1914 years. But there were serious underlying weaknesses which tended to overshadow the brilliant performance of industry in the 1920s. Psychologically and socially the war had left deep and ineradicable scars. The bourgeoisie had been shaken in its confidence, in its own belief in its right to rule, and its more sensitive members began to question as never before the foundations of a social order which could produce such heartless slaughter and misery. Even its hard-headed and flinty-hearted members were not unaffected. Despite the energy which went into reconstruction, and the industrial prosperity, it was inflation and the collapse of the franc which held the public attention. Inner changes had also taken place within the bourgeois class: new rich had arisen on the basis of war profits while many rentiers had suffered heavily from the default of the Russian and other governments and from the inflation. A prolonged crisis of confidence thus began, alleviated to some degree by the fact that the threat of revolution quickly subsided and by the prosperity of the decade. Poincaré's successful stabilisation of the franc in 1926 brought a feeling of relief from strain which lasted until the plunge into depression which began in 1931–32.

It was during the 'thirties, under the impact of the world economic depression, that the unresolved, long-term problems of French capitalism reappeared in a virulent form. They were combined, that is to say, with the inescapable results of an international conjunctural crisis more deepseated than any which capitalism had previously

5

experienced. The old historically moulded structures were now torn and strained as never before. Latent conflicts broke surface in a disturbing and politically violent form. Sections of the middle class turned to the extreme right, to the new forms of reaction modelled on fascism and national socialism. The peasants erupted under the leadership of loud-mouthed demagogues. The working class attained a new consciousness of its power and posed demands which were implicitly revolutionary. The old-line politicians grappled ineffectively with new problems which they did not understand and applied remedies which aggravated the disease. The economy declined and stagnated; it failed to generate spontaneous forces making for recovery and fell further behind the other industrial countries.

In the 'thirties the crisis of confidence spread and became endemic. It sapped the will of politicians and business leaders alike. Investment fell to new low levels. The class struggle reached a new pitch until, in 1936, the country stood on the brink of revolution. The experiment of the Popular Front failed to resolve the problems of French capitalism and, by endowing it with a legal forty-hour week, intensified them in the view of many observers. The franc had, after a five-year struggle, to be devalued. But devaluation, which might at least have permitted France to recover as well as other countries, had it been undertaken a few years before, did little to stop the decline. Although in some ways, because of under-industrialisation, France suffered less from the depression than other countries, this was hardly to the credit of French capitalism. In any case, although the challenge from the working class was resisted and government policy shifted sharply to the right after Daladier took office in 1938, the crisis of confidence was not resolved.

The swift military defeat of 1940, the humiliation of the armistice, the division of the country into an occupied and an unoccupied zone and the liquidation of the Third Republic closed an epoch. The rapidity and completeness of the downfall of the Third Republic was undoubtedly one of the most startling and unexpected events in twentieth-century history. More than a military defeat, it represented the culmination of a long process of inner decline and decay.

The examination of economic trends can shed some light on the factors which contributed to the catastrophe.

The war, and still more the defeat, marked the end of a chapter. A distinctive period in economic development was brought to an end. The problems of the 1940s and 1950s, though necessarily still reflecting the long-term structural influences, were in many ways qualitatively different from those of the pre-1940 era. For this reason the study breaks off at this point, at least until it can be resumed and brought closer to the present day.

The main emphasis in this work has been on the overall view. Rather than providing a factual record or a descriptive picture it selects for emphasis what seem to have been the most important determinants of change, growth and stagnation in the French economy during the period covered. There are important aspects of economic history upon which it barely touches, or treats only in a cursory way. In part this is because a more complete and empirical study would be impossible without an immense amount of spade-work in the primary and secondary sources. In part it is a matter of choice: there seems to be need for an approach of this kind which attempts to deal with the totality of economic development, with whole structures, and which makes hypotheses or draws conclusions which then have to take their chance in the course of discussion and debate. This method will not be to everyone's taste, but it can be said that in the literature of the subject it is a variety of writing which tends to be under-represented.

If there is not much stress on the principal economic actors and decision-makers as individuals, that is also partly deliberate. It reflects the view that the influence of particular entrepreneurs or politicians on the course of events was seldom decisive. The quantitative and statistical approach has also been avoided, partly because others have already made good use of it, partly because, however indispensable statistics are, they do not speak for themselves or even choose and arrange themselves. The hypotheses and explanations made here can be subjected to statistical verification in some cases; in others it is obvious that the appraisal has to be mainly qualitative and thus is as convincing as the general theoretical analysis of which it forms a part. In short, the attempt here is to provide an interpretative account of economic change in a broad setting. Within these limits this study may be of some assistance to those who wish to see French economic development in this period as a whole.[5] Perhaps the obvious lacunae and shortcomings will encourage others to enter this somewhat neglected field and take the explanation a stage further.

5. For a preliminary survey see T. Kemp, 'Aspects of French capitalism between the wars', *Science and Society*, xxxiii, no. 1, 1969. The survey made by C. Bettelheim, at the end of the Second World War, *Bilan de l'économie française, 1919–1946*, Paris, 1947, is interesting but not very accessible. For contrast see C. Gignoux, *L'Industrie française*, Paris, 1952, intended as a popular outline by a militant spokesman for the *patronat*.

2

BEFORE THE CATACLYSM: A PROFILE OF FRENCH CAPITALISM IN 1913

I

A varied geographical environment and a complex history made diversity rather than uniformity the outstanding feature of the French economic structure in the early part of the twentieth century. Regional differences and contrasts were still so great as to make national generalisations misleading if not actually meaningless. While some areas had gone through an industrial revolution which made them among the most advanced in Europe, others had stagnated with virtually little structural change for over a century. The national aggregates were thus dragged down by the presence of extensive underdeveloped regions in which there had been little technical progress or accumulation of wealth and in which, consequently, income levels remained low.[1] It is not the intention here to delineate in detail the economic map of France at this time. In the main the backward areas were in the south and west while industry had concentrated near mineral resources, around

1. According to P. Cornut, *Répartition de la fortune privée en France,* Paris, 1963, p. 411, private wealth *per capita* amounted to 16,684 francs in the Seine department, 9,384 in Seine-et-Oise and 9,128 in the Marne, the three richest departments, while at the other end of the scale it was only 1,190 francs in Corrèze, 1,143 in Lozère and 243 in Corsica in 1908.

the capital and the main ports and other nodal points. The differences between the two Frances were not simply of degree: they represented contrasts between centres of advanced capitalism and areas of rural backwardness into which entered many precapitalist traits.

The complexity of the economic landscape has perhaps been responsible for the varied appraisals which have been made of French development in the nineteenth and early twentieth centuries. From one standpoint the impression will be of slow, almost imperceptible growth so much outdistanced by what happened in other countries that it appears as stagnation or decline.[2] From another the picture is one of uninterrupted progress which steadily transforms France into an advanced industrial country and culminates in the brilliant performance of the pre-1914 decade.[3] Evidently, there are two sides to this process of national development which has to be grasped historically in its specific geographical setting.

Considered within a national framework every process of modernisation and industrialisation is bound to be uneven. Some areas are manifestly poorly endowed with the raw materials of industry and may, in addition, be condemned by soil, climate or topography to produce little in the way of an agricultural surplus. There may at the same time be social reasons why the human communities which make their living in these parts grow inordinately in numbers, thus eating up any increase in productivity and production made possible by improvements in technique or changes in the use of the land. It may be said, therefore, that the less developed regions in France suffered either from geo-

2. See, for example, D. S. Landes, 'The French entrepreneur and industrial growth in the nineteenth century', *Journal of Economic History*, ix, 1949; S. B. Clough, 'Retardative factors in French economic development in the nineteenth and twentieth centuries', *Journal of Economic History*, vi, 1946, Supplement; R. C. Cameron, 'Economic growth and stagnation in France 1815–1914', *Journal of Modern History*, xxx, no. 1, 1958; G. Boris, 'Les problèmes du développement économique de la France et leurs origines', *Politique Etrangère*, avril-mai, 1954; T. Kemp, 'Structural factors in the retardation of French economic growth', *Kyklos*, xv, 1962, Fasc. 2.
3. M. Lévy-Leboyer, 'La croissance économique en France au XIXe siècle', *Annales*, xxiii, no. 4, 1968; J. Marczewski, 'Some aspects of the economic growth of France, 1660–1958', *Economic Development and Cultural Change*, April 1961 and 'The takeoff hypothesis and French experience' in W. W. Rostow, ed., *The Economics of Takeoff into Sustained Growth*, London, 1963; F. Crouzet, 'Essai de construction d'un indice annuel de la production industrielle française au XIXe siècle', *Annales*, xxv, no. 1, 1970.

graphical or from social handicaps, or from both. Poor location in relation to the growing points of trade and industry at a time when transport improvements were taking place elsewhere could reinforce the isolation of some areas and widen the gap between the prosperous and the poor. If this was followed by the draining off of people and the decline of local activities, as the market became increasingly national and large-scale production developed in the more favoured places, the differentials could become still wider, even dramatically so.

There can be little doubt that this is what happened in France during the nineteenth century as a concomitant of industrialisation. The contrasts were made more apparent by the growth of towns and by that of Paris in particular, which is generally blamed upon political over-centralisation.[4] Nevertheless, national political unification had long been completed and the growth of French nationalism, as well as the establishment of a national system of administration, did something to attenuate the contrasts between the growing and lagging areas. No doubt it appeared at first sight as more of a difference between the town and the countryside than as a problem of economic dualism of the sort which the north-south disparities in Italy made inescapable. Regional underdevelopment was thus slow in being recognised as a national problem.

The existence of backward areas has to be explained not only in terms of geography, important as this is, but as a part of French social development. It is connected, of course, with the continued importance of the agrarian sector which also has to be explained historically. Only within this context can the characteristics of French industrialisation be understood and the specific features of French capitalism be distinguished. Because an attempt has been made to do this in some detail in an earlier work it will suffice here to make a summary profile emphasising the points which seem to be especially significant.[5]

4. J-F. Gravier, *Paris et le désert français*, Paris, 1958.
5. T. Kemp, *Economic Forces in French History*, London, 1971.

II

French economic history from the 1880s to 1914 is dominated by the thrust of industrialisation and modernisation into an economy still containing many archaic features. The revolutionary land settlement and the protracted industrialisation of the nineteenth century had retained in existence or failed to eliminate an oversized agrarian sector including many peasant holdings of small size and low productivity and a vast array of artisan and petty manufacturing units. As industrial capitalism established itself it did so to a large extent at first in the form of small or medium-sized family enterprises. It was, in any case, geographically concentrated in a few areas, leaving large areas of the country predominantly agrarian and economically undeveloped.

The characteristics of French agrarian society had issued from a long historical process under the old regime which had weakened the hold of the nobility on the land and strengthened the peasantry. The forces making for agrarian individualism remained extremely weak until the nineteenth century. By making its own revolution in and after 1789 the peasantry confirmed its hold on the land; it became a factor making for social conservation and at the same time constituted a barrier to the full penetration of capitalist relations into the agrarian sector. The preservation of peasant ownership, together with the division of property among the heirs on inheritance, meant the fragmentation, not the concentration, of land used in agriculture. A large proportion of the peasantry occupied, and generally owned, holdings which could do little more than provide for the subsistence of the family. At the same time the peasantry clung tenaciously to its property, and resorted to the restriction of family size in order to pass on its holdings as far as possible intact. The revolutionary land settlement, by strengthening individual possessiveness, thus contributed to the demographic pattern which was characteristic of France by the second half of the nineteenth century.

However, the picture must not be seen in static terms. Nor was the geographical picture at all uniform. There were regions of large estates and farming for the market, as in the cereal-growing areas of the Paris basin. In some, by virtue of the main product, there was specialisation and production of a surplus for sale: the traditional wine-producing areas are obvious examples. A given size of holding might be sufficient to establish a modest prosperity in one place while in another, less favoured by nature, it might not be adequate for a bare subsistence. Changes taking place during the nineteenth century—the coming of the railway, the growth of the urban markets and the rise in living standards and in expectations, the spread of education—undermined what remained of the old communal ties in the villages, intensified individualism and assisted the penetration of capitalist relations. This was a steady but uneven process which intensified regional contrasts and at the same time sharpened the differences between the country and the town. The rural exodus in the later decades of the nineteenth century pointed to the fact that, especially in the more disinherited regions, young men and women from peasant families were voting with their feet against the bonds of rural life.

The drift of population into the towns was assuredly held back in the earlier decades and still was reduced by the wide distribution of landownership. The prospect of acquiring land by inheritance, or of access to a holding through marriage, leasing or share-cropping, tended to hold men on the land and thus to limit the pace of recruitment of an urban proletariat. Although there is no overt sign that industry suffered from a labour shortage, the fact that population was kept on the land by the institutional structure must have influenced the character and rate of industrial development. It certainly helped to determine the character of the labour force. It meant, for example, that many workers still had a stake in the village: they might be seasonal workers or only go to the towns for a few years before they went back to inherit or help to work a family holding. They tended to regard their proletarian status as incomplete or provisional and they looked around in the towns for a place in petty commerce or some other activity which would haul them out of the working class. And, increasingly, the peasant ambitious for his son's future thought of making him a civil servant.

By the beginning of the twentieth century French population growth had become virtually stagnant (Table 1). From being the most populous European country at the time of the Revolution, France now assumed fifth place and had the slowest rate of population increase. More significantly this stagnation meant that France had the lowest proportion of young people and the highest proportion of the elderly. Between 1890 and 1913 the mortality rate exceeded the birth rate on seven occasions. The comparison with the still buoyant growth of population in other countries, notably Germany, was dramatic. The demographic problem, intensified by the effects of the First World War, was to assume central importance in the years to come.

TABLE 1. *French population growth (frontiers of 1871)—in thousands*

1872	36,103
1881	37,672
1891	38,343
1901	38,962
1911	39,605

Source: *Annuaire Statistique,* 1966

The slow rate of population increase affected the growth of the home market, reduced the gains from external economies, slowed the pace of demographic investment and produced an age composition which reinforced the authority of the mature or elderly in the family, in business and in politics. But it also reflected characteristics of economic and social development since 1789 which appeared to be irreversible. The emphasis on individualism and possessiveness encouraged the conscious control of family size among small property-owners. The main factor seems to have been the desire to conserve a patrimony and to pass it on if possible augmented and undivided. In a society of this kind children, or more than one or two, easily became an encumbrance. They stood in the way of individual achievement and ambition for the wife as well as for the husband. As each family—for it was the family which remained the basic social unit—took thought for its own future in an atomistic way, so a national population pattern was created with important repercussions for economic life. It was a France of only sons which was plunged into the demographic disaster of the Great War.

The slow reduction in the weight of the agrarian sector hampered the development of French capitalism but was at the same time a product of its character. After 1789 a compromise was tacitly made with the peasantry that it would at least be conserved. Through the nineteenth century the peasantry was seen as a socially conservative factor needed as a counterweight to the dangerous classes in the towns and as reliable electoral fodder for the local notables under the Third Republic. This did not prevent peasants from having to resort to mortgages or other forms of debt and little was done to assist the peasantry to help itself through the provision of credit, aid to co-operatives, rural education and other services. The backwardness of rural France was revealed more clearly as development took place elsewhere. No force came forward to change the rural balance either by a positive programme to modernise agriculture with peasant support or by accelerating the market forces undermining peasant self-sufficiency and favouring the large efficient units.

The protectionist movement during the agrarian depression of the 1880s was inspired by the industrialists and supported by the big agrarians whose incomes depended on the price of grain and other products.[6] Behind the tariff, however, peasant agriculture was able to survive to an extent which it might not have done without it. Once again, therefore, policy tended to conserve the status quo. It was, in any case, unimaginative and shortsighted. It helped to preserve those very features in the economy which held back the development of French capitalism and its adaptation to the changing needs of the twentieth century.

6. E. M. Golob, *The Méline Tariff: French agriculture and nationalist economic policy*, New York, 1944.

III

The picture from the agrarian sector and the provincial areas dependent on it for their economic life has to be reconciled with the impression of expansion in the decade or so before 1913 which is derived from the indices of industrial production.[7] It is precisely here that the contradictions and 'dualism' of French development emerge. Without a sudden period of accelerated growth corresponding to a 'take-off' the French economy had, during the previous century, assumed the character of an advanced industrial country. Industrialisation had begun on a limited scale in the eighteenth century and it had proceeded, after the interruption of the Revolution and the wars, more or less steadily, with some modest spurts of which that of the closing years of peace was among the most impressive.

What is outstanding at the beginning of the twentieth century, then, is the incompleteness of the industrialisation of France and the fact that it had been confined to a few areas of the country. At that time, and indeed for long afterwards, there was still a great potential for industrialising *extensively*: bringing industry to new regions and adding to the industrial structure from the existing pool of technological knowledge as well as by the development of new industries. The achievement of rapid rates of growth was possible under favourable conditions because there was a reserve of inadequately used labour power in the agrarian sector and artisan activities and a larger potential market once the surplus from agriculture could be increased and the division of labour carried forward as a result of the development of industry itself. Sections of the capitalist entrepreneurs of this period did begin to grasp these possibilities and create a modern industrial sector based on advanced technology.

---

7. 'Les années qui précèdent la guerre marquent un tournant dans l'histoire française. Les taux de croissance industrielle sont en hausse très sensible: 2·66% de 1885 à 1905, 4·42% entre 1905 et 1913 (1·93% et 4·19½% pour la production industrielle, bâtiment inclus). Bien plus, le produit global par tête, qui est la mesure la plus proche que nous avons pu calculer pour suivre le revenu réel par tête, est en net progrès.'—Lévy-Leboyer, *op. cit.* p. 799.

The question which arises is why this had not been done before, or only so incompletely. The severe judgements passed on the French entrepreneurs in the nineteenth century, while not undeserved, have to be qualified by an understanding of the environment which created them, and with which they had to deal.[8] All the conditions of the economy which have been outlined tended in the typical industries of the first stages of industrialisation to make the French entrepreneur cautious in his approach and to limit his horizons. Often the market he confronted was limited and grew slowly, or he was handicapped by inadequate raw material supplies or other factors which raised his costs. From the start French industry was at a disadvantage because British firms had built up a substantial lead, particularly in cheap machine-made goods, had pre-empted the lion's share of world trade in these products and could compete in its own home markets. The reaction in the main was defensive and protectionist, but not entirely so. French entrepreneurs sought out profit opportunities in fields in which they had a special advantage, which had been neglected by their foreign rivals, or which had been opened up by the growth in incomes in the more advanced areas of the world.[9]

French industry thus proved itself most successful in fields closest to the consumer, where quality and finish were the key to successful selling. In this it carried on a tradition from the old regime and exploited the prestige which French products had acquired with the wealthy at that time. Income distribution was no less skewed in the bourgeois societies of the nineteenth century and, with growing wealth, the market for high-class, semi-luxury or luxury

8. It is interesting to note that the strictures on French businessmen and their methods made by American economic historians in the 1950s echoed those made by German officers investigating French industry during the occupation in 1916. Using the industries in Germany which they knew as a standard of comparison they found that French industry was backward in scale, technique, financial methods, extent of vertical integration and concentration. They attributed this to the predominance of the family firm, even when organised as a joint stock company, and to the rentier mentality of the French businessman who 'aime à se retirer des affaires dans la force de l'âge et à depenser ses revenus à Paris ou sur la Côte d'Azur'.—'*L'Industrie en France Occupée* (translation of the German enquiry, published in 1923), p. 437.
9. See M. Lévy-Leboyer, 'Le processus d'industrialisation: le cas de l'Angleterre et de la France', *Revue Historique*, ccxxxix, no. 2 1968.

goods was a growing one. Industrial tradition made it particularly easy for French industrialists to follow this path and to harness the new techniques to quality production. In addition, of course, much of this type of production continued to be carried on by isolated artisans or putting out workers, or in small workshops. This added, once again, to the complexity of the industrial structure and makes generalisation difficult.

In the older industrial centres the small family enterprise continued to prevail in the early twentieth century. It typically depended on its internal sources of finance and thus had no need to resort to the capital market or the banks. This was the old-style capitalism which could continue to flourish as long as general conditions remained favourable and which had considerable powers of survival. It had, and needed, a protected home market and a cheap labour supply, was little interfered with by the public powers, whose support it could always call upon in the case of a labour dispute, and it was lightly taxed. Such conditions were not exclusively French, they were found in most of the older industrial countries. They did, however, conserve features which had become archaic and built into the economy an inflexibility to change which could prove a serious handicap as time went on.

IV

The main indications of rapid change came at this time in the building up of a large-scale metallurgical industry and the pioneering of some of the new industries of the twentieth century. One of the most remarkable economic developments, and one which began to affect the structure of French capitalism as a whole, was the establishment of a modern steel industry based on integrated plants in that part of Lorraine ore fields which remained French.[10] The

---

10. Important in this regard was the availability of the Gilchrist-Thomas process. As M. Lévy puts it in *Histoire économique et sociale de la France depuis 1848*, Paris, 1952, p. 230; 'Les facteurs qui retardent l'économie française, manque de matières premières et manque de capitaux, n'existent plus pour l'industrie lourde. La France dispose de fer. Les entreprises métallurgiques disposent de larges capitaux. Il y a là les bases d'une transformation radicale de l'industrie lourde et de sa localisation.'

heavy capital investments required in the new techniques and the high risks involved brought about concentration of control and dependence on new forms of finance. Joint stock companies had to be formed; even wealthy family businesses had to look to the capital market; and new and intimate relationships were established between heavy industry and the big banking and financial institutions. The shifting of the base of French capitalism towards heavy industry had important political and economic consequences which were not to display themselves fully until after the First World War. It threatened the old equilibrium in French society established during the nineteenth century. In the meantime it showed itself in a new-founded expansion, a new business dynamism in contrast with the old-style capitalism which still held sway over large sectors of industry.

The development of French capitalism had largely been the work of a number of great financial and industrial dynasties, supported by a growing industrial and commercial bourgeoisie and resting on a wider base of prosperous peasants and small property owners. Thus wealth was both unequally distributed and dispersed in the hands of large numbers of modest savers. Established industry in the main supplied most of its own financial requirement from reinvested profits. The rentier sought a safe outlet for his savings or was attracted by the prospect of capital gains. At any rate there was a large pool of savings to be tapped and as established business was not able or willing to make use of it the banks and the stock exchange did. In this way financial entrepreneurs came forward, looking for profitable opportunities, and succeeding in directing rentier funds both into financing the large-scale projects of advancing capitalism at home and abroad and into the loans of foreign governments.[11] Paris thus became a great financial centre and France became second only to Britain as an international creditor.

Although the French economy was less outwardly-oriented than the British its character was nonetheless formed by its relationship to the world economy. Reference

11. This process has been traced in detail by R. C. Cameron, *France and the Economic Development of Europe*, Princeton, 1961.

has already been made to the effect on French industrial development of Britain's priority. Foreign trade thus sought channels which were not directly competitive with Britain and later Germany. Exports tended to be the more highly finished manufactured products: luxuries or semi-luxuries, wines and foods too expensive for mass consumption. Thus exporters sought out markets in the high income urban markets of the civilised world rather than in the less developed countries. Much French trade, of course, went overland and did not, therefore, provide traffic for the mercantile marine; in any case, shippers did not have the benefit of outgoing bulk cargoes of the sort which their British competitors found in coal. Despite subsidies the shipping industry languished.

As a manufacturing country France was dependent on vital imported raw materials, including coal. As an agricultural producer domestic prices were sensitive to world market trends. Indeed, every step forward which the economy made drew it into deeper involvement with the world market. Although few French people emigrated, the country was a great and growing attraction for foreign tourists and already, to a certain extent, for permanent immigrants. Tourists' expenditures thus made up an important invisible item in the balance of payments and encouraged investment in such fields as hotels, restaurants and casinos. Tourists also bought many manufactured items, especially those which bore the cachet of quality and which were made, in all probability, by artisans or petty manufacturers. In this way, too, France's peculiar relationship to the outside world helped to strengthen certain traits in the domestic economy.

Still more significant was the growth of foreign lending which made France the second largest creditor country holding approximately $8,700 million abroad. This was a result of two main factors—the existence of a large, passive lending or rentier population made up of the urban middle class and the more prosperous peasants, and the role of the big financial institutions, firstly the old established *haute banque*, mainly Parisian, and then the deposit banks founded in the second half of the nineteenth century in the provinces as well as the capital. Investible funds owned by people with no direct access to remunerative outlets, plus a tradition of large-scale finance, issued in a flow of funds to foreign countries in search of profitable returns. Thus, while most sectors of industry seemed to suffer from a shortage of capital and whole areas of the country remained undeveloped, the most sophisticated techniques were being used to channel French savings abroad.

The financial entrepreneurs who controlled the business of foreign investment were by no means somnolent or buried in routine.[12] On the contrary, they showed themselves most active in searching out new borrowers and in enlisting support from the press and politicians for their activities. Indeed, they were able to present it, despite some opposition on the grounds that home industry was being deprived of capital, as of national importance. French bankers had always preferred to deal with large-scale borrowers, especially governments. They were not anxious to immobilise resources in long-term investment in industry. The banking houses promoted foreign loans on terms very favourable to themselves; they were little concerned with what happened afterwards or what rate of return the investors received on their money. In any case, in the period before the First World War they were operating in a bull market, playing for a rise as their predecessors had done under the Second Empire. But it was a source of potential weakness that about 75 per cent of French foreign lending went to governments and most of it to Central and Eastern Europe and the Middle East. It had, therefore, a definite political flavour. It was intended to bolster French security against the threat from the Dual Alliance.[13]

12. Thus R. Girault, says: 'Avant 1914, des banquiers, des industriels ont osé entreprendre à l'étranger; menant au loin une politique audacieuse et de vaste envergure, ils furent des "entrepreneurs" même si leur réussite a été mesurée, même si leur destin parait parfois chancelant à la veille des hostilités. Un renouveau des méthodes bancaires, des personnalités dirigeantes, conduit le capitalisme français hors du territoire national; l'investissement direct occupant une place plus large dans l'exportation des capitaux témoigne des tendances volontaristes des capitalistes français, de leur esprit d'entreprise.'—'Pour un portrait nouveau de l'homme d'-affaires français vers 1914', *Revue d'histoire moderne et contemporaine*, xvi, 1969, p. 349.
13. Especially after 1910 German economic expansion became increasingly menacing for French interests: German products built up a strong position in the French market, and, to jump over the tariff wall, raised in that year, branch plants were

French financial imperialism was less successful in the colonies proper.[14] Territorially large, the French empire was in many respects a disappointment to its promoters: it was costly to acquire and to develop, and the immediate returns were not impressive.[15] Some interests in France undoubtedly profited from colonial expansion and development and actively supported it. Contractors built railways and other parts of the infrastructure to open up colonial territories for trade. The colonies offered sheltered markets for French exports and became important sources of supply for certain raw materials. Marseilles and Bordeaux built up a substantial trade with the colonies. Administrators and army officers and many humbler functionaries found scope for their ambitions, and secure pensionable jobs in the empire. If there remained a net loss which the taxpayer had to meet, that is not to say that many private interests did not gain or that it could not be easily written off to France's 'civilising mission'.

French imperialism, after all, was very much in the image of the domestic economy and the society which built it. Taking the earnings from foreign investment and the relationship with the colonial empire as a whole French capitalism did have something of a *rentier* character. While it did not depend literally on tribute, the income from past savings invested in the colonies and foreign countries was an important part of the revenue of many middle-class Frenchmen. The institutions of French capitalism were also closely bound up with manipulating the income flows to which colonial enterprise and foreign investment gave rise and ensuring the reinvestment of earnings outside the country. This pattern was firmly fixed and unlikely to change in the short run. It made up part of the distinctive physiognomy of French capitalism in the prewar era. There

established in France. 'Aux appétits expansionnistes des milieux d'affaires allemands, la France oppose une réaction défensive'.—R. Poidevin, *Les Relations économiques et financières entre la France et l'Allemagne*, Paris, 1969, p. 819.

14. 'French capital exports are invested mainly in Europe, primarily in Russia (at least ten billion francs). This is mainly *loan* capital, and not capital invested in industrial undertakings. Unlike British colonial imperialism, French imperialism might be termed usury imperialism'—V. I. Lenin, *Imperialism: the Highest Stage of Capitalism*, Moscow, n.d., p. 107.

15. H. Brunschwig, *Mythes et réalités de l'impérialisme colonial français*, Paris, 1969.

is, therefore, no point in speculating about what might have happened had more capital been invested at home, particularly as there is no evidence that industry was willing to borrow more than it was already doing from outside sources.

V

Despite the centralised character of the state under the Third Republic and the considerable ramifications of its administration, public opinion and policy were fashioned by the doctrines of economic liberalism. The functions of the state were to provide for external and internal security, to uphold the sanctity of contracts and to provide certain essential services for the public which private enterprise was unable or unwilling to provide. The funds required to finance these activities made it necessary to raise revenue by taxation and by other means, which included a state monopoly of the production of matches and tobacco. It was no part of the state's function otherwise to intervene in the economic arena, except to ensure that the laws of the market were permitted to operate as freely as possible. Faith in individual enterprise and the virtues of economic liberty were never higher than in the years immediately before the First World War.

That does not mean, of course, that the state's activities had no economic influence. In fact they deeply affected the lives of every citizen through taxation, education, conscription and its law-making and law-enforcing powers in ways which were wholly or partly economic. The state was a large employer; the employment it offered in its offices or services was secure and pensionable, with prospects of advancement through a graded hierarchy. While posts at the top of this hierarchy offered security, material reward and status to the bourgeois social élite and were therefore sought after, perhaps more eagerly than a career in business, the life of a functionary had undoubted attractions for more humble folk. Security and pensionable employment became a goal which many members of the peasantry and the middle class sought for their sons. It corresponded to a certain distaste for risk and uncertainty which these classes displayed in other spheres of life.

The state maintained a large conscript army and, as war approached, its military expenditure rose. The economic burden of compulsory military service must have been considerable. It may have had demographic as well as economic effects. It meant in any case a diversion of man-power from productive employment which had to be supported by the community at large. War expenditure also meant lucrative contracts for some entrepreneurs, especially the large firms concerned with the production of steel and munitions. It therefore raises the question of the political influence which these firms may have exercised during the pre-1914 years, the relations which may have existed between the contractors and the politicians.

If the state appeared to be enormously powerful because of the weakness of intermediate institutions between it and the citizenry, the account of what it did not do is impres-sive. It intervened little if at all between employers and workers, who did not acquire a legal right to organise until 1884. There were factory regulations, but they were less comprehensive and less well enforced than in Britain and Germany. The French employer remained very much the master of his plant and of his labour force; the only responsibilities he had were virtually those he chose voluntarily to accept. On the whole, he resisted bargaining with trade unions as much as he did the interference of the state with his right to do what he liked with his own.

VI

Again, before 1914 the state provided little in the way of social services and nothing which compared with the social security system in Germany. It was assumed that most of the emergencies of life, sickness, old age, unemployment, widowhood, loss of parents and so on, would be taken care of within the family, by charity or by the local authorities. This was an important lag which was not to be filled even during the interwar years. The impression of laisser-faire capitalism in this era is confirmed if the tax system is examined. What stands out here is the dependence on indirect and traditional taxes and the strong resistance to successorial duties and especially an income tax. The former, when imposed at a modest level, were denounced as expropriatory, while an income tax was not accepted until the eve of the First World War. The defects in the tax system were to make the financing of that war more difficult and thus contributed to the undermining of the franc during and after it.

Is it possible to point to the defining characteristics of French capitalism on the eve of the First World War? It is tempting to do so with a few words: France was an old, rich, mature capitalist country, second in rank as a colonial power and an international creditor. On the surface the dominant trends were stability and prosperity. The franc had been a safe money for over a century.[16] Savings were high and there was confidence in the future. Industrial production was surging forward at a rapid rate. For the middle class, at least, times were good and the period has earned the description of *la belle époque*.

That this was not a full or an entirely accurate picture should be clear enough. The industrialisation of France remained incomplete and left a large part of the economy in the grip of stagnation and stunted development. The real meaning of the 'equilibrium' between industry and agriculture, which some writers pointed to with pride, was that an excessive proportion of the population was tied to back-breaking and poorly rewarded work on the land and that the average *per capita* income was consequently dragged down. Primarily as a result of the excessive weight of agriculture in the economy all kinds of archaisms were conserved. These traits were obviously dominant in some areas although in others they had all but disappeared. Sharp geographical contrasts mirrored the unevenness of French development over the previous century and a half.

If part of France still lived under conditions which had

16. The silver value of the franc had been fixed by the law of 17 Germinal of the year xi (1803); in practice it had gone over to a gold basis after 1878. There had been periods of monetary crisis (1848, 1871) but they had been shortlived. By the 1900s the franc was considered by the public to be as fixed a quantity as the metre or the gramme.

scarcely changed in any fundamental way since the eighteenth century, another and growing part had long been drawn into the orbit of advanced capitalism. Large-scale enterprises, integrated concerns, close connections between industry and the banks, a modern industrial proletariat and the landscape of modern industrialism characterised this sector. Here the old competitive forces were losing out to the new tendencies of 'monopoly capitalism'. Patterns of urban living and consumption were likewise spreading as the population balance shifted steadily towards the towns.

However, the industrial proletariat still remained a minority of the population and a substantial part of it continued to work under the old conditions in small factories or workshops. The peasantry, the artisans, the small traders and professional people, conserving a modicum of independence and owning a certain amount of property, continued to act as a powerful counterweight to its influence. Economically it would not be correct to speak of their activities as being 'precapitalist' since they were drawn into a market economy and in many ways made up an essential part of the structure of French capitalism at this stage. Nevertheless they represented the earlier phases of its development and constituted a barrier to its adaptation to the pressures of the twentieth century.

In retrospect the vulnerability of the French economy to war stands out very markedly. Despite the brilliant rates of growth in industrial production achieved in the previous years, France had fallen behind Germany in aggregate economic power over several decades. The disparity of forces had become overwhelming. The slowing down of population growth, coupled with the fact that German population continued to expand, was to show itself in terms of the manpower which could be mobilised for military and industrial purposes during the war. The French industrial structure was weak in certain lines of production, such as chemicals, machine tools and instruments, which were of military significance. Agriculture was to face a manpower crisis and a shortage of fertilisers and feeding stuffs. The distribution of the main industrial areas also increased France's military vulnerability and in fact those in the north and east were to be overrun or turned into battlefields. France could only wage a twentieth-century war as part of a coalition which was as much economic as it was military. If that was not clear beforehand it was a truth which rapidly imposed itself once the conflict began.

3

THE ECONOMY AT WAR[1]

I

The economy of France, as well as her administrative
machinery, was not prepared for a war of the duration and
intensity of that which began in 1914. Though war itself was
not unexpected it was believed that modern economies
could not support a long conflict.[2] Civil and military
leaders assumed, therefore, that it would take the form of
sharp decisive battles between the armed forces. Military
preparations were made accordingly and no question arose
of economic mobilisation as a necessary corollary to the
mobilisation of the nation's able-bodied manpower into the
armed forces. It was regarded as sufficient to constitute a
stock of armaments and supplies, declare a state of siege,

1. Much useful information on the French war economy is to be found in the volumes
published under the auspices of the Carnegie Endowment for International Peace.
Mostly written by academics, politicians and leading civil servants, who had access to
vital information, they suffer from a lack of analysis and perspective, emphasising
mainly the legal and administrative aspects. However, these works and the many
others generated by the war, make the period 1914–20 probably the one most
intensively studied in French economic history. That is not to say that a satisfactory
or definitive study has yet been produced. See J.-B. Duroselle, 'Bilan et perspectives
économiques de l'Europe', *Revue d'histoire moderne et contemporaine*, xvi, no. 1,
1969.
2. A view generally held and not confined to France. The economic corollaries of
mobilisation sketched here were general to the belligerent countries.

requisition the means of transport and other items as needed and leave the general staff to secure victory.

These assumptions prevailed in the atmosphere of patriotic euphoria in which mobilisation was ordered on the outbreak of war in August 1914. What had not been expected was the economic paralysis which followed, and emergency measures had to be taken to deal with the situation. The banks suspended cash payments and a moratorium on debts was declared.[3] The government took powers to fix prices, ration supplies and make payments to the families of soldiers who found themselves without resources or employment. From the first, therefore, the involvement of the state with the economy became inescapable and it was soon to become still more widespread and systematic.

In the meantime, the proclamation of the state of siege handed over the main decision-making powers to the military authorities.[4] The heavy machinery of mobilisation ground forward, snatching men from their civilian jobs, and especially from the land, conveying them to the military depots and on to the front or to other posts. The railway network, which played an indispensable role in this process, became immediately subject to state control and the employees of the companies were mobilised in their existing posts.[5] The need for state control of the railways had been recognised before the outbreak of war: it was one of the few forms of economic mobilisation which had. It was some time before the realisation dawned that the railways were a pointer to what would have to be done in industry. The very interruption to normal transport and communications flowing from the concentration on shifting men and supplies for the war imposed further controls in any case.

In the first weeks of the war the interests of the economy were wholly subordinated to the needs of the front. The generals had taken command, the politicians had tempo-

3. Though this did not apply to the use of bank deposits by firms working on war contracts.
4. P. Renouvin, *The Forms of War Government in France*, New Haven, 1927, especially ch. 2.
5. M. Peschaud, *Politique et fonctionnement des transports par chemin de fer pendant la guerre* Paris, n.d., p. 56.

rarily abdicated, the operations of a free market economy had been dislocated, and the result was industrial chaos. Factories, mines and essential services were stripped of their able-bodied workers and had to close down or reduce their activities to a fraction of normal. This meant that many workers below or above military age and those exempt from military service, as well as many women workers, found themselves unemployed and facing destitution.[6] It meant that the pipelines were not being filled up either to supply the military machine or to provide the needs of the civilian population. The logic of the situation was to drive the government into a directing role in the economy which it had not envisaged and on which it was reluctant to embark.

The social and economic problems rapidly assumed critical dimensions. In Paris and the main towns unemployment figures soared in the summer of 1914 as economic activity slowed to a snail's pace. Not only did many small or medium-sized enterprises have to close down because owners and key personnel had been called to the colours, but larger plants vital for the maintenance of war supplies were not spared. Renault's motor works in Paris, not yet the giant it was to become but nonetheless important, was denuded of a large part of its labour force and production was reduced to a trickle. The same happened in all the main industrial centres: production was grinding to a halt. At the same time a labour reserve of abnormal size was brought into being side by side with a chronic scarcity of skilled and experienced workers who had been indiscriminately mobilised to the army. The question of a planned distribution of labour power, so completely ignored beforehand because of a failure to understand what a war between industrial nations would be like, now became basic to the continued pursuit of the war.

The slowing down of production, the requisitioning of supplies for the army and the militarisation of the transport system necessarily meant shortages in the civilian sector. A

6. In August 1914 there were 600,000 unemployed in Paris and the department of the Seine, according to A. Fontaine, *L'Industrie française pendant la guerre,* Paris, n.d., p. 49, and while 25 per cent of the labour force was mobilised, another 40 per cent was unemployed. The problems involved are discussed in greater detail in the specialised monograph published under the auspices of the Carnegie Endowment, *Chômage et placement* by A. Crehange.

banking moratorium was imposed which temporarily paralysed the normal flow of credit. The normal working of a market economy was disrupted from all directions. To complicate the economic problem still further, the onrush of the invading German armies engulfed the industrially crucial areas of northern and eastern France. The national economy was soon deprived of a substantial part of its capacity in coal-mining, iron and steel, engineering, textiles and many other industries which were of vital importance for carrying on the war as well as supplying the civilian population.[7]

This drastic curtailment of industrial capacity, together with the fall in production as a whole, made the French war effort dependent on supplies from Allied sources and thus soon began to introduce a factor which was to be of great significance after the war—inter-Allied war debts. The balance of forces in Europe as a result of the industrial development of the previous three-quarters of a century, especially the rise of Wilhelminian Germany, had placed France at a grievous disadvantage in the carrying on of a modern war. Despite her own growth, her relative 'backwardness' was a factor of great, perhaps fatal, military significance. France could no longer fight a continental war singlehanded. Supplies from overseas, especially products of advanced industry, which could not be paid for by exports or by the realisation of assets held abroad, were necessary if defeat were to be avoided.

II

New policies were required to meet the exigencies of the war. It soon became a question of survival in which old shibboleths derived from the free market economy would have to be abandoned. A unique and dangerous situation existed which required the intervention of the state as a

---

7. The losses represented 53 per cent of coal production, 64 per cent of pig iron, 62 per cent of steel, 60 per cent of cotton and substantial proportions of capacity in a wide range of other industries. The occupied areas had produced prewar about one-fifth of the country's wheat supply and one-quarter of its oats. Beet sugar production and refining were especially hard hit. About one-third of food-processing capacity was in the occupied areas.

coordinating and directing force. This was evident as it became clear that the war would at least continue into 1915 and later that preparations would have to be made for a war of long duration. The new form of warfare, which followed the early indecisive stage of a war of movement—the stalemate war of the trenches in which the rival armies slogged it out over months or years—required munitions, especially shells, in quantities never before imagined. Simply to keep the war going a large munitions industry had to be built up. Industry was set the overriding task of supplying the needs of trench warfare, and especially the voracious demands of the artillery; henceforth the only limit to output was that of capacity.

To feed war industry massive quantities of raw materials and fuel had to be obtained from domestic and foreign sources. Transport facilities had to be geared to the requirements of war industry. Above all workers had to be found to man the war plants. The mobilisation of labour became as essential as the mobilisation of soldiers for the front; without the output of industry the front could not be supplied and would collapse. The blanket mobilisation of the early days of the war now had painfully to be undone.[8] Men had to be brought back from the armies to use their skills in the war factories and other sources of labour supply had to be found. At the same time it was necessary to safeguard the supplies of the civilian population both on grounds of morale and in order to permit war workers to obtain adequate supplies of food, fuel and other essentials. More and more the rear was drawn into the war effort. Had this been foreseen an apparatus of controls could have been established in advance. In fact, new administrative organs had to be established *ad hoc* to deal with the problems as they arose. Parallel to the growing demands of the war and the operations of government went the problem of providing the financial means for the acquisition of supplies on government account and for the payment of administrative personnel.

8. The question of labour mobilisation is dealt with in a number of the Carnegie monographs including Crehange, *op. cit.*; W. Oualid and C. Picquenard *Salaries et tariffs, conventions collectives et grèves*; R. Picard, *Le Syndicalisme devant la guerre*; M. B. Nogaro, and L. Weil, *Main-d'oeuvre étrangère et coloniale*; and M. Frois, *La Santé et le travail des femmes pendant la guerre*.

The war rapidly imposed a series of interrelated problems on the attention of policy-makers. It must be emphasised that they presented themselves separately and by degrees, and they were handled piecemeal as they arose. The French approach, perhaps surprisingly, was essentially empirical. An apparatus of controls and new administrative organs was built up, which grew in complexity from 1915 onwards, but it did not do so in response to any pre-conceived plan or intention. It is proper to speak of it as an exercise in improvisation carried out with some reluctance, and only under the pressure of overwhelming circumstance —the threat of military defeat—by men whose whole background and experience had been with a freely operating market economy in which the interference of the state was kept to a minimum.[9]

Capitalism in war was not the same thing as capitalism in peace. The market was to a large extent superseded and its place was taken by the state as a main purchaser and as co-ordinator of distribution. It might have been thought that there was enough support in French history for this to be grasped and accepted readily as soon as war was contemplated. In fact it was not so. The tradition of Colbertism was operating weakly before 1914 and the experience of previous wars seems to have been largely forgotten. What predominated in the minds of politicians, economists and businessmen was the theoretical and practical virtue of unhindered market forces. The French Revolutionary legislation and the Napoleonic Codes had laid the juridical basis for a capitalist economy based on the free market economy. The state had a legal obligation to maintain private property rights and market freedoms. The wartime contingencies provided for had not envisaged an economic war between the great industrial powers, but a short sharp war of the old type. The minds of politicians and of legisla-

9. 'The invasion of state control was not premeditated. There was not, at any rate in France, any attempt, when once the certainty of a long war was established, to lay down systematically the program of the State's progressive intervention. The steps were taken under the pressure of circumstances, from hand to mouth, as the need arose. But this empirical development was continuous, from 1915 to 1918' Renouvin, *op. cit.* p. 53. But, as he goes on to say, 'By the operation of successive measures, private enterprise disappeared under the encroachments of State control; it was regulated, disciplined, and stifled. The economic regime fell foul of "individual liberty" in practically all its manifestations' (p. 54).

tors adapted themselves only slowly to the entirely new conditions confronting them.

What stands out in the first phases of the war, therefore, is the reluctance of the administrators to intervene in the economy, their continued respect for market forces, their unwillingness to interfere with property rights. When they intervened they did so under pressure of overwhelming emergency, to deal with an exceptional situation, conscious that they were contravening economic laws or taking measures which they would not have been legally entitled to take under peacetime conditions. In the field of distribution and consumer rationing this reluctance was particularly marked.[10] The financial measures adopted showed the same tendency. On the whole, therefore, there was no shift in the opinion of politicians or the bourgeois public regarding the proper spheres of the state and private enterprise. That the state was drawn more and more deeply into economic matters was imposed by necessity and accepted with some reluctance even then. There was no sign of a break with the prevailing orthodoxy; the war was a special case and its lessons were not understood.

The politicians and administrators were ill-equipped by the past experience and their intellectual baggage—heavily loaded with the dogmas of classical political economy—to grasp at once the exigencies of war in the age of industrial power and mass society. They can hardly be blamed for not being able to transcend the prejudices of their class and time. Certainly, however, their slowness and unwillingness to think through the problems made the creation of an apparatus of wartime controls a laboured process and limited its completeness and effectiveness. Through to the end reliance continued to be placed as far as possible on the market, but the movement towards control and even planning was irresistible; the alternative was to perish. Under the pressure of the war and the threat of defeat the march towards state intervention and the centralised allocation of resources went implacably forward as an objective process. Reluctantly and empirically, in one

10. P. Pinot, *Le Contrôle du ravitaillement de la population civile*, Paris, n.d. Allocation of bread and sugar by ration cards did not take place until February 1918 in Paris and June for the rest of the country.

sphere after another, the government was forced to take measures which modified or abrogated the hitherto sacrosanct market forces. This was the sheer logic of modern warfare, which no capitalist economy could resist; in France it was certainly not envisaged or planned beforehand, nor was it much reflected upon at the time.

A pressing problem which had to be dealt with within a matter of weeks after the outbreak of the war was that of the allocation of manpower. It became increasingly evident that the production worker was as indispensable for victory as the front-line soldier. Only a mighty industrial effort could turn out the war material of all sorts, particularly ammunition and shells, in the increasing quantities which the fighting men required. Moreover, artillery, vehicles, machine guns and all forms of ordnance and mechanical equipment could only be produced under the most advanced industrial conditions. What was required was large scale production of standard lines in unprecedented quantities: the emphasis was on advanced technology, mechanisation and rational organisation of production. Labour had to be made available in the required quantities and with the requisite combination of skills. In these regards France was at a considerable disadvantage compared with the larger and more advanced industry possessed by Germany. The loss of ten of her most advanced industrial departments which were occupied by the enemy or rendered useless by being in the battle zone was a further severe blow.

The initial impact of the war was to create an overall labour surplus. Many enterprises, large or small, closed their doors or continued to produce at only a low rate owing to the call-up of key personnel, the disorganisation of transport and supplies, the uncertainty about markets and the restriction of bank credit. Employers themselves left for the army and, if they could find no one to carry on the business, that also meant the closure of the workshop or factory. In the towns, therefore, a pressing problem of unemployment rapidly emerged alongside industrial stagnation. Unemployment lasted well into the following year among men outside the military age groups called up, those exempt and women. To them were added the many thousands of refugees who poured in from Belgium and the occupied departments.

Public provision thus had to be made for the unemployed as well as the refugees, who included many able-bodied people available for work.[11] Maintenance payments were made and offices were set up to act as labour exchanges, though there was nothing really corresponding to an organisation of the labour market. At first the administration chose to deal with problems as they arose, locally and on a piecemeal basis. Since many peasant holdings as well as larger farms had been stripped of their male labour a drive was made to recruit some of the available labour to help with the harvest in 1914. But these were short-term measures which offered no solution to the main problem, which was soon to be that not of labour surplus but labour scarcity.

The scarcity of skilled manpower was a direct consequence of unselective conscription. It became acute as industry turned over to war production and the demands of the front increased imperiously. In this sector, then, a shortage of labour, and especially of skilled labour, rapidly appeared. Since practically all the skilled men of military age had been swept into the army in the early days of the war it became necessary to comb the camps and military depots in order to draft back into the factories many workers whose services with a lathe or drill could be more useful than with a rifle and bayonet.

In making possible the mobilisation of labour for war industry the trade unions played a key role.[12] Although only a minority of French workers belonged to unions many more no doubt heeded their instructions. The most articulate sections of French labour before the war, organised in unions affiliated to the *Confédération Générale du Travail*, were committed to a belligerently antiwar and antimilitarist policy, and this was true of the most promi-

11. About 600,000 refugees (154,298 from Belgium) received government assistance in 1914–15; another 283,661 were unassisted.
12. Picard, *op. cit.*: 'Il exista, pendant toute la guerre, des liens étroits entre le gouvernement et les syndicats ouvriers, pour l'oeuvre commune que poursuivait le pays et pour la sauvegarde des intérêts ouvriers' (p. 76).

nent trade union leaders and militants as well as of the politically conscious workers. The government fully anticipated that on the outbreak of war it would face a mass campaign of strikes and sedition, and to forestall this the police had compiled lists of active trade unionists, socialists and anarchists who were to be arrested as a precautionary measure, known as '*Carnet B.*'[13]

In fact, as war came closer in July 1914, a confused situation prevailed in the working class movement. Although antiwar resolutions had been passed by the unions as well as by the Socialist Party few had faced up to the hard reality of whether it would actually be possible to act upon them. The fact that at this time the working class was in a descending phase of militancy and the confusion following the assassination of Jaurès, the prestigious socialist leader, helps to account for the mood which prevailed in the working class.[14] In fact, although it is difficult to speak of enthusiasm for the war in the working class, there was more than an echo of Jacobin nationalism to be heard in the response to the swelling tide of nationalism and anti-German feeling generated by the press and official organs. Most of the leaders and militants in the trade union and political wing acquiesced in mobilisation.

The government shrewdly estimated that to take action against all the leaders scheduled for arrest in '*Carnet B*' would be the most likely way of stirring up working-class resistance to the war. The powers vested in the prefects by the state of siege effectively curtailed democratic rights and liberties, including trade union activities, and stifled any opposition that there may have been.[15] Within a very short time most of the trade union leadership as well as the majority of the Socialist Party agreed that the *patrie* was in

13. Picard, *op. cit.*, pp. 51–3. For a recent discussion based on police records, see A. Kriegel, *Aux origines du communisme français* Paris and The Hague, 1964, i, 57 *seq.* and n. 3. An order was sent to the prefects on 1 August 1914 not to proceed with the arrests. Some militants were, however, arrested, including about 150 in the north and the Pas-de-Calais.
14. The situation in the working class immediately before and on the outbreak of war has excited considerable controversy which is still going on. See, for example, Kriegel, *op. cit.*, and G. Haupt, 'Guerre ou révolution' in *Temps Modernes*, no. 281, December 1969 and the literature cited.
15. As Millerand put it in addressing delegates from the Fédération des Métaux, which represented engineering workers: 'Il n'y a plus de droits ouvriers, plus de lois sociales, il n'y a plus que la guerre.'

danger and accepted collaboration with the state in dealing with the problems of war production.[16]

The first of these was to decide which of the men called to the colours, by reason of their possession of special skills in short supply in war industry, should be released to the factories.[17] From September 1914 industrialists could visit military depots and select from the conscript soldiers those they considered suitable to fill vacancies in their plants. This procedure continued to be used until May 1915. In the meantime a government department was set up, forerunner of the Ministry of Armaments, to which wider powers were granted. By the *loi Dalbie* men subject to call up for military service could be allocated instead to work in war factories.[18] The trade unions were drawn into collaboration with the government in operating these and similar measures. During 1915, and until the end of the war, trade unionists sat on mixed commissions with employers' representatives to decide which mobilised soldiers should be released to war industry. The metal workers' union had a role of particular importance in ensuring the successful functioning of industrial mobilisation. It was, in fact, an essential part of the *Union Sacrée* that the trade unions should be drawn into close cooperation with the state and with the employers. It is difficult to see how the manning of war industries, and the necessary dilution of the labour force and relaxation of trade union restrictions which went with it, could have been successfully and smoothly carried out without the cooperation of the trade unions.

In practice the union leadership, apart from a minority which was at first small, decided officially that the class struggle was in abeyance for the duration as far as they were concerned and that it was necessary to cooperate with the state in the organisation of the labour market. Their actual conduct during the war turned out to be a drastic reversal

16. See, for example, G. Lefranc, *Le Mouvement syndical sous la troisième république* Paris, 1967, pp. 186–212, for the attitude of trade union leaders during the war. Léon Jouhaux, secretary of the *Confédération Générale du Travail*, became a *Commissaire à la Nation* and joined the government in Bordeaux. Of the leading figures in the CGT few retained an antiwar position.
17. The direct responsibility engaged by the unions in these respects is fully dealt with—approvingly—by Picard.
18. This law was drawn up after consultation with trade union leaders such as Merrheim. Picard, *op. cit.*, p. 68.

of what might have been expected from their previous statements. If the unions did not achieve as much power in industry as they did in Germany or Britain this was largely a result of the previous weaknesses, not of unwillingness to cooperate with the state. And they did, in any case, make what the leadership regarded as important gains as a result of their change of front.

The men who were released to the factories still remained subject to direction and military discipline, though it was necessary, on trade union insistence, to pay them according to the recognised scales.[19] By the second year of the war an all-round labour scarcity was apparent which could not be met simply by release of men from the forces, especially as the growing demands of the front for manpower also had to be met. It was necessary, therefore, to look elsewhere as war production mounted, new factories were built and war-induced industrialisation spread to areas of the country where there were few wage-earners with settled habits of industrial work. Large numbers of women were brought into the labour force for the first time, or to take up work in the factories and public services from which they had hitherto been excluded.[20] Jobs were found for able-bodied refugees, prisoners of war and wounded soldiers. Members of peasant families migrated to the towns to enjoy the high earnings of war industry. And the net was cast wider still as the government set up an agency to recruit foreign workers, not only from neighbouring countries but from as far away as China, as well as encouraging many to come from the colonies.[21]

19. According to Oualid and Picquenard, *op. cit.*, p. 153; 'Ils étaient civils à l'usine, ils relevaient de l'autorité militaire au dehors.' They were restricted as to residence, use of bars, etc. as though they were members of the armed forces: 'Ils relevaient disciplinairement, en dehors du travail industriel, de l'autorité militaire et étaient soumis à la jurisdiction des conseils de guerre' (p. 155).
20. Frois, *op. cit.*
21. Nogaro and Weil, *op. cit.* The number of foreign workers involved varied from period to period. They give the following for the total of colonial and Chinese workers:

North Africans: 132,321
Indo-Chinese: 48,955
Madagascans: 4,546
Chinese: 36,941
                   ───────
                   222,763

The advantage with foreign, and still more with colonial immigrants, was that they could be directed to any part of the country where labour was required—not only to war factories, but to the battle zone, hydroelectric and other constructional sites, etc.

Naturally, most of the new recruits to industry lacked the requisite skills or even familiarity with factory work. The pressure of labour scarcity, especially of skilled labour, led to machinery and workshop organisation in the war industries being adapted to the possibilities of the labour force. Tasks formerly performed by skilled men were broken down into their component parts and performed by machines operated by unskilled or semiskilled workers after the minimum of training. The tendency was to establish continuous flow production based on the maximum proportion of this semiskilled, rapidly trained labour.[22] It was on this basis that the number of women in the factories greatly increased. A general process of 'dilution' took place in parts of the metal trades especially which had hitherto been preserves of skilled men. The tendency at first was to work the newcomers as hard as possible by stepping up the hours of work and increasing the intensity of the labour process. The trade unions opposed this tendency as far as they could and pressed for equal pay for equal work and the maintenance of established labour conditions.[23] However, many workers recalled to the factories were still subject to military discipline and might be brought before a Council of War if they went on strike. The restrictions on trade union rights limited the field of action of the unions and many, if not most, of the newcomers to industry lacked any tradition of organisation.

On the other hand, the very scarcity of labour strengthened the hands of the trade unions. The concentration of workers in large plants and the arduous conditions which prevailed offered a field for organisation and also made it necessary for the employers and the government to find a bargaining agent to assist in disciplining the labour force. The weight of the trade unions tended to increase, but only as part of the administrative machinery of the state.[24] The government sought to preserve social peace and to avoid strikes and disputes which could hold up production, although as war weariness spread in the closing years of the war discontent tended to grow and 'wildcat' strikes broke

22. Fontaine, *op. cit.*, pp. 175 seq.   23. Picard, *op. cit.*, pp. 95 seq.
24. Picard, *op. cit.*, Lefranc, *op. cit.*, both apologists for trade union policy during the war, do not use the phrase, 'part of the administrative machinery of the state'. But this is what is involved in the policy of *présence* defended by Jouhaux.

out. The trade unions were able to carry on wage bargaining with the employers and to draw up with them collective contracts which received the endorsement of the government. They tried to protect wage standards by insisting on equal pay for equal work, hoping thereby to prevent women and foreign workers from being used to depress wages after the war or to confront the returning soldiers with the threat of unemployment. In short, the wartime role of the unions proved to be quite different from that which their main leaders had envisaged before 1914. The prewar 'revolutionary syndicalism' had turned into an industrial recruiting agency for the war machine.

IV

Despite high money wages earned by some munitions workers and the reports of working class extravagance in the press read by the middle class, there can be little doubt that working class living standards deteriorated during the war. In the first year or so, under the impact of high unemployment, wages of many workers in employment fell and thousands were in fact living on public relief. As conditions in the labour market became more straitened, that is to say from the latter part of 1915 and during 1916, money wages began to rise and the climb continued on a more sharply ascending curve in the last stages of the war and until 1920 when the postwar boom broke. The cost of living began to rise at about the same time and seems to have outdistanced the increase in money wages, so that the average real wage actually fell in 1917 and 1918 and indeed in the first postwar years.[25] In short, the evidence clearly

25. It is assumed that real wages rose in the last quarter of the nineteenth century by about one-third and then held their own between 1900 and 1913, see J. Lhomme, 'Le pouvoir d'achat de l'ouvrier français au cours d'un siècle: 1840–1940', *Le Mouvement Social*, no. 63, avril–juin, 1968. Unfortunately this article does not deal with the war period. According to J. Singer-Kérel, *Le Coût de la vie à Paris de 1840 à 1954*, Paris, 1961, the average weekly wage of a Parisian male worker fell during the first three years of the war, rose in 1917 but fell in 1918 to reach the lowest point for the period 1913–39 in 1920 at the end of the postwar boom; see pp. 147–50. However, it is possible that wage increases in Paris were less than those in other towns. Picard, *op. cit.*, concludes as follows: 'Dans l'ensemble, les salaires diminuèrent en 1914 et 1915, se relevèrent legèrement à partir de 1916 davantage en 1917 et montèrent assez vite de 1918 à 1920. Mais le coût de la vie, surtout dans les centres ouvriers, progressait

shows that, on the average, real wages were below their 1913 level through to 1920. This does not take into account, of course, the hardships, shortages and insecurity resulting from the war and the postwar situation or of the increased intensity of work which characterised production in the munitions plants. The best that the unions were able to do in this situation was to prevent standards declining still further.

There are other costs borne by the working class during the war which cannot be measured and some deterioration was inevitable owing to the fall in production, the virtual cessation of new house building and the other direct consequences of the war.[26] It may be said that workers in the rear suffered less than front-line soldiers, did not risk death and earned considerably more. Because more workers were exempted from military service or released for war work the working class provided proportionately fewer victims than the peasantry or even the professional middle class. Such comparisons have only a limited value. The working class was, in any case, not a fixed entity. New strata were being recruited to it during the war. For many, no doubt, the movement to the factories represented an improvement in real income as would be the case with peasant and foreign recruits. The numerous army of women workers who went into the war factories came to a large extent from the families of workers who had been conscripted. The trade unions therefore fought to maintain wage standards on the grounds that they were defending the interests of workers still in uniform who would one day return to industry.[27] Labour scarcity gave the working class a certain bargaining position of which they made increasing use as patriotic

---

plus rapidement encore. . . . Pendant toute la durée de la guerre, les salaires réels restèrent inférieurs à ce qu'ils étaient en 1914' (p. 113). Evidently, given the great variety of conditions among different strata of workers, there were categories whose real wages did rise and others who lost more than the average.
See also P. Louis, *La Condition ouvrière en France depuis cent ans* Paris, 1950, who concludes: 'De 1914 à 1918, on peut dire qu'il y eut une régression de la condition sociale. Elle était inévitable dans la crise que le pays traversait. Les vivres faisaient défaut. La masse de la population était obligée de comprimer ses besoins. Les soucis matériels étreignaient des millions d'individus. Si des enrichissements rapides et scandaleux étaient acquis par les spéculateurs, ceux qui travaillaient de leurs mains voyaient se réduire leurs ressources' (p. 75 and the whole of ch. 6).
26. Rent control may have done something in the opposite direction.
27. Picard, *op. cit.*, pp. 95 seq.

enthusiasm evaporated and a sense of grievance and discontent took its place.

Wartime conditions of scarcity and inflation scarcely
made possible anything but a compression of consumption
for the main body of the working class. Many goods were
unobtainable or in short supply and rationing remained
mainly by the purse. Stories of extravagance on the part of
allegedly highly paid munitions workers rested no doubt on
the fact that only certain forms of consumption were
available to spend money on, including some particularly
conspicuous ones. Partly this arises from the incompleteness and unsystematic nature of wartime controls. Many
inessential or luxury articles continued to be produced.
The government was unwilling to undertake a fuller
direction of industry or introduce more comprehensive
rationing. It continued to rely, as far as possible, on market
forces. The rise in prices, the continued availability of
inessentials and luxuries, at a price, rationing by the purse
and the appearance of scarcities created a sense of deprivation and grievance which fed the growing discontent in the
later stages of the war and the immediate postwar years.

Strikes in war factories began to pose some serious
problems in the course of 1917, year of the Russian
revolutions and the army mutinies, when war weariness
began to take its toll.[28] The government responded by
turning to the trade unions again, bringing employers and
unions together and sponsoring collective agreements
which the unions would then have some responsibility for
enforcing. In the war industries proper mixed arbitration
committees were established in an attempt to avert shut-
downs. Shop delegates were also to be elected in the factories: their role being to act as intermediaries between the
workers and management and to deal with shop-floor
grievances.[29] They never played much of a role during the
war.

The government desired above all to preserve industrial
peace and maintain war production. It thus became
involved in wage bargaining on a purely empirical basis,

28. See, for example, Picard, *op. cit.*, pp. 204–32; Kriegel, *op. cit.*, 154–67; and M.
Gallo, 'Quelques aspects de la mentalité et du comportement ouvriers dans les usines
de guerre, 1914–18', *Le Mouvement Social*, no. 56, juillet–sept., 1966:
29. Oualid and Picquenard, *op. cit.*, pp. 420 *seq.*, Picard, *op. cit.*, 123 *seq.*

looking to the trade unions as convenient partners in establishing industrial discipline. This policy had a limited success until it was threatened by more generalised discontent.

V

The essence of the changeover from peacetime to wartime production was a drastic change in the product-mix and the destination of output. Industry had to be geared to providing the munitions and supplies necessary to carry on the war.[30] This meant in part that different things were produced, in part that commodities formerly sold on the market to private consumers were produced to government order for the consumption of the armed forces. But the civilian sector had also to be supplied, still mainly through the market. The government was also a spending agency, buying what it required in the market and in some cases requisitioning supplies. The outcome was not planned but was an empirical compromise of government intervention and market forces. Government demand became the imperative factor in the use of transport and scarce materials. The civilian sector thus experienced shortages and prices tended to shoot upwards. In response the government moved in to control prices and regulate the distribution of essential goods; the production of less essential and luxury items became more difficult and more expensive.

From the first the wartime administrators endeavoured to work as far as possible within the market framework on the basis of cooperation with businessmen.[31] Private management as well as private ownership thus continued to

30. Indeed there was an enormous increase in the output of munitions: production of 75 mm shells which the Ministry of War had estimated at 10,000 per day in case of war reached 300,000 in May 1917; production of rifles rose 290-fold, that of machine guns 170-fold. Besides supplying the French army, large quantities of war material were sent to Serbia, Russia and Roumania and much light as well as some heavy artillery was supplied to the American army, Fontaine, *op. cit.*, p. 378.
31. Mainly through the medium of the 'Consortiums' which, amongst other things, distributed raw materials purchased by the state to the users at fixed prices. These bodies disappeared after the war, but according to one authority their passing was regretted in some business circles, see C. J. Gignoux, *L' Industrie française*, Paris, 1952.

be the rule over most of the commercial and industrial scene. The market also survived, but its role as a means of allocating resources was greatly restricted. The industrial firm no longer necessarily had the right to produce what it considered would be most likely to sell at a profit and to sell where and to whomsoever it pleased. The state stepped in to a growing extent from an early stage in the war to control the supply of labour, fuel, raw materials and transport facilities and to allocate them according to its own scale of priorities determined not by ability to pay but by the needs of the war effort. Moreover, it appeared on the scene as a consumer armed with plenary powers to demand what it chose on behalf of the war effort. The war became a major and overriding end of production to the extent that the state acted in this way.

In other words, by its requisitioning, control of supplies of certain raw materials, imposition of price ceilings and, above all, its contracts with private industry, the state gave imperative shape to the composition of final output while leaving a field clear within which market forces continued to operate. This output had a price; a substantial part was purchased directly by the state which taxed the public or used its credit for the purpose, or indirectly with incomes paid out by the state and derived from the same source. However, since ownership and control of industry remained almost entirely in private hands, and since the administrators of the war economy accepted and respected the rights of property, important bargaining counters remained in the hands of private enterprise. The exigencies of war, if anything, strengthened its bargaining position.

The voracious and clamant needs of the war machine for supplies, sensitivity to public criticism of any publicised failure to provide the front-line fighters with adequate supplies of munitions and other equipment, reduced the ability of those negotiating on behalf of the state to drive hard bargains. This meant, in practice, that war contracts were drawn up laxly and that the scale of payment to suppliers was usually generous and often excessive. It was, almost, production at any price. Part of the penalty of improvisation, and perhaps of civil service ignorance of industrial conditions, was loose or non-existent costing of war contracts.[32] Industry no doubt delivered the goods (there were some exceptions even to that rule) but it was not easy to see where the lines were drawn between patriotism, normal business profits and 'profiteering'.

This was one reason, and not the least important one, why the financial costs of the war greatly exceeded anything previously imagined, requiring public spending on a wholly new and unprecedented scale. In this, of course, France shared the common experience of all the belligerent countries. The question was how this vast outlay on the war could be financed.

VI

The financial question, like the others connected with the war, was approached at the beginning on the assumption that the war would be short and with a complete underestimation of the scale of the military operations. Partly in deference to the military, partly out of a desire not to antagonise the public, methods of financing the war were chosen which could not fail to have inflationary consequences. As has been seen, financial considerations took a secondary place on the spending side. Lax or inefficient administration, lack of control by parliament or the usual publicity through the press and other channels, all made inevitably for waste and excessive cost at all stages. The mistakes made in financing these outlays were no less costly. The historian of French war expenditure stated bluntly that: 'The financial policy of France during the Great War of 1914–18 will remain a model of what *should not be done*. A worse financial administration it would be difficult to conceive.'[33]

The attempt to finance the war by expedients which would not disturb too drastically the peacetime ways of doing things or squeeze the recipients of higher incomes

32. See G. Jèze, and H. Truchy, *The War Finance of France* New Haven, 1927, pp. 119 *seq.* (A translation of the independent monographs—G. Jèze, *The War Expenditure of France,* and H. Truchy, *How France Met the War Expenditure*—which appeared separately in French under the auspices of the Carnegie Endowment). It is admitted that there was much waste and squandering; prices tended to be monopoly prices and the most efficient firms levied a 'rent' at the expense of the state.
33. Jèze, *op. cit.,* p. 112.

was at the root of the serious monetary difficulties which France was to experience after the war and whose social and political consequences were to be incalculable. The reluctance to resort to direct taxation followed from the struggle against the income tax which the conservative moneyed interests had waged before the war. After lengthy discussions in parliament an income tax law had been finally passed in March 1914 but the tax only became operative in 1916 and did not make a substantial contribution to the revenue until after the Armistice.[34] The lack of an established and accepted income tax, with a proper system of administration, and the failure to impose one on an emergency basis, proved to be a serious handicap in the financing of the war. As French citizens already paid relatively high indirect taxes, it meant that the government was thrown back mainly on borrowing to meet the heavy and growing financial drain of the war.

French war finance was thus inherently inflationary. It was based on heavy borrowing from the banks and from the public which, in turn, used existing assets as collateral in order to subscribe to war loans.[35] The government was confronted with an imperative need to provide means of payment in order to keep the front supplied. As it passed out war contracts so manufacturers and suppliers resorted to the banks to get their paper discounted in order to obtain cash to pay wages and other expenses. There was a considerable expansion of banking services during the war —it might almost be said that the banking habit became established at this time—but it involved a process of credit creation which, however effective as an instrument of industrial mobilisation, was bound to force up prices. Eventually, too, it brought the risk of the degradation of the currency itself as the volume of paper grew at a time when the supply of goods available on the civilian market inevitably contracted.

The old canons of financial orthodoxy were held in abeyance more from timidity than from recklessness. Policy showed a complete poverty of invention and pro-

34. Truchy, *op. cit.*
35. The government borrowed 16,000 million francs from the Bank of France, 22,000 million from the sale of *bons de la défense* and 55,000 million by long-term public loans.

ceeded by expedients, too frightened to disturb established habits by draconian measures. The alternative, with the country on an inconvertible paper currency from the outbreak of the war, was predictable. There was a steady inflation only kept within bounds by exhortations and direct controls. As Dulles has pointed out, there was a fairly close correspondence between the growth in the note circulation and the rise in prices, though this does not mean that there was necessarily a causal relationship between the two.[36] Unless the government was to make inroads into income by direct taxation the steady inflation was the price which had to be paid in order to command the resources needed to pursue the war. Inevitably this led to problems while the war was on and stored up even more serious problems which were to explode in the postwar depreciation of the franc.

Purely financial measures were not adequate to enable the voracious needs of the war machine to be met. The state had therefore to enter the field of production itself both by providing massive assistance for the conversion of private plants to war production and by setting up new munitions factories. Such intervention was not only a breach with past practice and orthodox opinion but it required changes in the law because the government only had the right to make payments 'for services rendered' and not to make advance payments to private firms as it now had to do.[37] By stages the government was driven into deeper involvement with war industries. Until the summer of 1915 it contented itself with making advances to industrialists for raw materials and wage outlays. From the September of that year it began to advance considerable sums for the creation of new factory space and it went on to participate still more completely in furnishing the capital investment required for war plants. State intervention thus went forward as an inexorable process.

---

36. E. L. Dulles, *The French Franc: 1914–1928*, New York, 1929, p. 107; note circulation rose by about 300 per cent, prices by 350 per cent.
37. Truchy, *op. cit.*, ch. 3.

VII

As the war went on the relationship of the state to the economy assumed a new form broadly comparable to that in all the belligerent countries. The state organised the flow of material required for the war effort, purchasing the entire output of the most advanced sectors of the economy according to contracts and prices largely determined in advance. It became the financial backer to war industry, enabling it to obtain short term finance from the banks, and itself furnishing part of the fixed capital required. A substantial part of final product was thus paid for by the state and it was from this payment that industry had to repay the credit it obtained. As inevitably happens in a war economy, incomes were created in industrial production and ancillary services to which there was no counterpart in the shape of an increased flow of consumer goods on to the market. On the contrary, this flow was curtailed to make way for war production and was severely hit, in any case, by the loss of industrial capacity resulting from enemy invasion. In the course of the inflationary spiral which was set in operation price increases tended to outstrip the rise in money wages which resulted from the buoyant labour market. Price controls, piecemeal rationing and appeals to patriotism moderated the price rises to some incalculable extent but the inflation steadily built up.[38]

As the war dragged on into 1917 and 1918 so the consequences of the financial laxity of the earlier years became more apparent. Now there was no time or opportunity to make a change. The demands of the front had become still more inexorable and any major departure in financial policy was out of the question.[39] Furthermore, as the

38. Wholesale price index, annual average: 1913 = 100:

1914 (3rd quarter)	116·8	1917		315·2
1915	163·7	1918		401·8
1916	215·5	1919		406·9

Source: Jèze, *op. cit.*, p. 110.

39. On this point see the discussion by Truchy, *op. cit.* who concludes 'to suppose that the French war finance might have been quite different from what it was is unquestionably an illusive view of the past. . . The severest taxation could not have modified the economic conditions that the events of the war had imposed on her' (p. 215).

public's lending capacity was not infinite, so the Ministry of Finance sought other methods of covering its requirements. In short this meant resort to the printing press: an increasing volume of paper money was put into circulation to meet the government's needs. The inflationary pressures built up still more strongly against the wartime barriers. For the present these barriers still held up. Public confidence in the money had not been undermined. There were more pressing concerns than the value of the franc and no doubt most people assumed that the rise in prices was a temporary phenomenon. The battle for the franc did not begin in earnest until the more deadly battle at arms was over.

French financial methods, born of the purest orthodoxy, proved more costly than they need have done and stored up immense problems for the future. In the meantime the laxity of the state meant handsome gains for many industrial firms. Contracts were drawn up and costed on generous terms. They permitted the building up of industrial capacity (some, of course, not easily adaptable to peacetime purposes) and the accumulation of monetary reserves which became available for investment after the war. In the case of a few firms which were badly managed or fraudulent the state received nothing in the way of supplies for the outlays which it made. As a whole manufacturing industry was in a strong bargaining position during the war and made the best of it. For those capitalists who made honest tax returns some part of their windfall profits was scooped back in taxation.[40] The rapacious methods of profiteers were frequently denounced during and after the war. No doubt the profiteers of which the press spoke were a small minority. Much more important was that large sections of industry, especially in munitions, engineering and similar fields, did well out of the war by strictly fulfilling their contracts and doing nothing to draw public criticism.

If the war saw the rapid growth or even the beginning of some industrial fortunes, it also meant an inordinate growth in the National Debt which grew still larger, as will be seen, in the period of postwar reconstruction.[41] This became an

40. The law of 1 July 1916 levied a tax on exceptional war profits.
41. Interest charges on the Public Debt, which stood at 1029 million francs in 1913, were 7610 million francs in 1919 and continued to increase in the following years: Truchy, *op. cit.*, p. 117.

important factor in undermining public confidence once people had time to think about it. At the same time, also ominous for the future, there was a depreciation, as yet still relatively modest, of the franc on the foreign exchanges. These results of inflation, with their adverse public consequences, had favourable results for some. The diminution in the real burden of debt, which followed from the fall in the value of money, clearly favoured big industrial and commercial borrowers. On the other hand, the rentiers of the middle class and the upper bourgeoisie were open to loss unless they were able to compensate elsewhere. The repercussions of inflation and its social consequences belong, however, chiefly to the postwar period. The point is that it took its origin in war finance; failure to grasp the nettle there and then made its sting exceptionally potent at a later stage. Indeed, the war brought to a close a long period of currency stability identified with the *franc germinal* and opened an epoch of monetary troubles which shook the social and political framework of France throughout the interwar period.

VIII

Confronted with the threat to national survival involved in the struggle with Germany the government was obliged to supersede the market mechanism in order to allocate supplies in accordance with the needs of the war effort. This required the establishment of a system of controls and priorities and the development of new administrative techniques. Intervention by the state, despite its many imperfections, could not be avoided; the involvement of the state with the economy and the carrying through of industrial mobilisation as a corollary of military mobilisation arose from the very nature of modern war.

The necessity for some state action early became necessary in order to relieve the distress provoked by the blanket mobilisation of able-bodied men. An unemployment fund was created and labour exchanges (*bureaux de placement*) were set up to make displaced workers available to employers—a more rational organisation of the labour market which continued prewar trends.[42] More important as an innovation was the drafting of men already mobilised to their military units, or eligible for service, into the war factories. It had to be recognised that wars could not be won by armies alone and that the supply of munitions, and indeed a large part of industry, had to be organised as a military operation. Only the state possessed, or could acquire, the plenary powers necessary for this purpose.

Economic organisation for war required new forms of international cooperation with France's allies. Imports of food and raw materials as well as war supplies were necessary if France were to remain in the war. This raised problems of procuring and shipping these commodities to France, and of paying for them. Joint arrangements were entered into and credits had to be obtained as the loss of important industrial areas, as well as the needs of war, drastically curtailed exports and other sources of foreign exchange were also severely cut.[43] A drive was made to undertake production at home of commodities which had formerly been imported, especially of those like chemicals, which had come from enemy sources.

There was bound to be a drastic reduction in supplies available to the civilian market. Labour and raw material scarcities greatly reduced the amount of constructional activities not directly related to the war effort. The output of luxury industries also suffered in this way, but the pressure was indirect and not a deliberate result of a policy of industrial concentration. Thus certain inessential articles continued to be produced all through the war, at a price. An effort was made to keep some of the export trades going so that they could earn foreign exchange or maintain goodwill in foreign markets but shortage of shipping space made this increasingly difficult as the war continued.

The apparatus of regulation and control developed piecemeal, as a response to a growing problem of scarcity and the need to establish an order of priority in the allocation of resources and the distribution of goods. French administrators proved reluctant to interfere with market forces. As

42. Crehange, *op. cit.*
43. Imports, by quantity, were well maintained while exports fell off through loss of markets and shortage of supplies; see the summary in Fontaine, *op. cit.*, pp. 142 *seq.*

far as possible businessmen were brought into the administration of controls affecting supplies to industry as well as with the allocation of imported raw materials purchased on government account. The organisation of the war economy took place in a haphazard, empirical fashion, and not as a deliberate exercise in central planning. The administrators preferred methods which conserved as much as possible of the market and which could be operated through established channels of trade. Thus control of prices was used rather than rationing. The actual apparatus of control remained inadequate.

Many of the problems of wartime in fields such as labour supply, public health and housing, food distribution and rationing, were dealt with as far as possible on a local rather than a national basis. Instead of imposing a nationally uniform system of administration the central government laid down the main requirements and provided funds where they were necessary but considerable initiative remained in the hands of local authorities. This decentralisation could be justified on two grounds. In the first place, these authorities, especially in the towns, had an administrative apparatus while the state had none. Secondly, it permitted account to be taken of the great differences which existed between one part of the country and another—between Paris and the rest of the country, between the urban areas and the country and between the war zones and the areas well clear of the front. It was, perhaps, the best way of eliciting local support and initiative under wartime conditions and given the deep suspicion of state intervention prevalent in the middle and upper classes. On the whole, outside the war zones, the war brought few drastic changes in the apparatus or methods of administration.

IX

The war amputated a substantial part of France's industrial capacity both in heavy industry and in a wide range of consumer goods. It was impossible to make good the lost production from the northern and eastern departments occupied by the enemy or in the war zone. Nevertheless there was some recovery in aggregate production as the result of the building up of capacity elsewhere. Industrialisation was greatly speeded up in regions such as the southwest which had been scarcely touched by modern industry before 1914. The industries which expanded most were those such as iron and steel, engineering, vehicle and chemical industries directly geared to the war effort, industries which were also, for the most part, the backbone of technologically advanced industry. The war thus assisted the development of the modern, advanced sectors of French capitalism, those which were the most highly developed technically and organisationally.[44] The conditions of wartime expansion brought these growing sectors into contact with the banks to a greater extent than had hitherto been common in French industry. The exigencies of large-scale, highly mechanised production, all the new problems involved, undoubtedly did much to break down old habits and rigidities in industry and in business methods generally. In this sense the war helped to drag the French economy into the twentieth century faster than might otherwise have occurred.

One aspect of this was the elimination of many smaller firms and the accelerated concentration of control. The smaller firms suffered through the calling up of their proprietors or of leading personnel. They were the worst hit by lack of financial reserves and the stringency of credit; indeed by all the difficulties of carrying on business in wartime. Government contracts were mostly for huge quantities of standardised articles which the larger and better-equipped firms were best suited to fulfil. Such firms, often with government backing, expanded their plants or set up entirely new ones to produce war supplies. In many fields the most that the smaller firms could expect would be a share of the subcontracting to which big government orders gave rise. Thus the process of industrial concentration, discernible already before the war, was given a definite push forward and the trend was to become still more marked in the 1920s.

---

44. Fontaine, *op. cit.*, pp. 175 *seq.* Kriegel, *op. cit.*, p. 362, 'Terrible paradoxe: cette guerre tueuse, cette guerre dévastatrice, cette guerre ruineuse fait aussi accomplir un formidable bond en avant à l'industrie française'.

Thus it can be said that war and reconstruction contributed powerfully to the modernisation of French capitalism. Modern, technically advanced industries were carried into new regions which underwent, in wartime, their own 'industrial revolution'. New contingents were added to the industrial proletariat from the villages and small towns of hitherto backward areas. To cope with the unprecedented needs of war heavy capital outlays were made on modern, highly mechanised equipment which could be operated by these unskilled recruits to the labour army. In the large war plants especially, intensive use was made of scientific methods and managers and technicians became familiar with 'Taylorism' for the first time.[45] The mass production lines contrasted with the old traditions of French industry but in many fields they began to conquer.

At the same time, wartime scarcities encouraged a search for substitutes and innovations to save fuel or material. For example, the loss of the coalfields in the occupied areas and restrictions on imported supplies resulted in economies in the use of coal in the iron and steel industry and in thermal power stations. Even more important was the stimulus which the shortage of coal gave to the development of hydroelectric power.[46] The significance of this for the long-run growth of the economy hardly needs to be demonstrated. It opened up a new industrial prospect to hitherto agrarian regions and provided the basis for new industries in the electrometallurgical and electrochemical fields. Progress was made too in expanding the output of synthetic chemical products such as dyestuffs and pharmaceuticals to make good the German imports which had now been cut off.

Despite the deterioration in working-class living standards, mainly a result of a fall in the real wage, and the obvious hardships suffered by people in the occupied and devastated areas, civilian supplies were well maintained. Food supplies on the whole were adequate, with only partial rationing resorted to in the closing stages of the war. Civilian industries, even some producing inessential or

45. Fontaine, *op. cit.*, p. 176.
46. Which the French, conscious of their shortage of coal, called *la houille blanche*. See M. Blanchard, *Les Forces hydro-électriques pendant la guerre* Paris, n.d.

luxury commodities, were kept going with women and children. Retail trade, able to obtain such commodities and benefiting from the rising prices, remained prosperous. As the war went on, however, shortages began to make themselves felt and prices rose more rapidly. The growth of discontent in the towns and the strikes of 1917–18 were a response to these adverse changes, but they also indicated the relative lack of hardship, or even inconvenience, experienced by the civilian population until then. It was the moral effect of the mounting toll of casualties which left few families untouched and the fact that no end to the war seemed in sight, which affected the morale of the civilian population more than any material deprivation. And then, in the last heave of the conflict, with the arrival of American troops in strength, supply difficulties increased, the transport system became overburdened and the fact of scarcity was brought home to the civilians in the shape of rationing, food shortages and soaring prices.

Into the economic balance sheet of the 1914–18 years enter a number of factors which assisted France to meet the ordeal of a long and grinding war without chaos or collapse, despite the loss of valuable industrial and mining areas. In the first place certain vital supplies were ensured by co-operation with her allies and obtained without counterpart payment at the time.[47] This economic contribution of France's allies was a *sine qua non* for her continuance in the war. It made it possible to provide for the needs of the fighting front without imposing too harsh a burden on the civilian population. Secondly, the weight of agriculture, though a handicap in gearing the economy to war production, and itself afflicted by scarcity of manpower, fertilisers and other aids, enabled food supplies to be maintained. This was important in view of the submarine campaign against

47. By the end of 1919 France had contracted foreign debt to the extent of 43,583 million francs (conversion of foreign currency values at the mean exchange rate for each year). By this means France was able to pay for essential supplies of all kinds without which she would have been unable to equip and arm her forces and to feed her population under wartime conditions.

Allied shipping in the second half of the war. The agrarian sector also, of course, provided a reserve from which was drawn a disproportionate part of the manpower for the trenches which was consumed at such murderous rate. Thirdly, given these conditions, it was possible to devise, by piecemeal measures, a system of controls which was acceptable to the public without imposing intolerable hardships or restrictions and yet sufficiently effective to enable the war to be waged successfully.

In this connection it seems necessary once again to insist on the empirical manner in which the government extended its role in the war economy. At every stage the politicians acted with reluctance, under pressure of circumstances, improvising as they went along. They dealt with problems as they arose, exercising little foresight or anticipation of the problems to come. They did not grasp the wholly new issues raised by industrial mobilisation to meet the exigencies of twentieth-century total war. What is instructive in the wartime story is the way in which 'objective conditions' imposed themselves on the decision-makers. The result was a series of expedients to meet particular situations and emergencies as they appeared.

It is thus hardly possible to speak of wartime 'planning' in France; even in the final stages the economy was never fully geared to the tasks of war under central direction. The involvement of the state with the economy had not been thought out or prepared for in advance. It arose out of the necessities of the time and it was kept within limits by men whose whole experience and training had been with a market economy and who had the usual liberal prejudices against state intervention. The obligations assumed by the state were thus regarded as temporary and unpleasant necessities to be brought to an end as soon as possible. If there were some businessmen who later looked back with nostalgia to the position they had held in the wartime system of controls, the overwhelming preference was for a rapid and complete return to a free market system as soon as possible after the war. There was no continuity between wartime and postwar policy except in so far as the government assumed financial responsibility for reconstruction arising out of the war itself.

4

COUNTING THE COST[1]

I

France emerged from the war as a victor power: the *Union Sacrée* thus received its consecration. Political and military leaders identified with victory conserved their prestige and the ruling class as a whole retained its self-confidence. Although not impervious to the revolutionary shock-waves which were sweeping Europe in the wake of the Bolshevik Revolution, French society tended to resume its prewar forms which, in politics and administration, had not in any case been much changed during the war. As in the other belligerent countries there was a general belief and desire that somehow there could be a return to normalcy, to the pre-1914 situation, seen after over four years of ruthless bloodletting and upheaval in a nostalgic glow.

The persistence of the old forms and the relative weakness of the threat of revolution, or even of big social changes, conceals the cataclysmic effects which the war had on French society. Below the surface a myriad processes

1. There is no pretension here to draw up a balance-sheet of the costs of the war. This has been done in a succinct form by A. Sauvy, in *Histoire économique de la France entre les deux guerres* Paris, 1965, vol i., ch. 1. See also the work of Jèze and Truchy, cited p. 46, n. 32, and for war losses, M. Huber, *La Population de la France pendant la guerre* Paris, 1931.

were set in motion which profoundly affected social relations and attitudes. Nothing, in fact, could be the same as before. The history of the interwar period is very much that of the working out of the consequences of the war crisis. While physical damage could be repaired and the economy reconverted to peacetime needs, nothing could bring back the dead, nor could the mental scars left by the war be readily removed. However, only the material costs of the war can be measured and even this task raised innumerable difficulties for those who undertook it. The wider consequences of the war are open to wide differences of interpretation.

The war cut a swathe through the male population larger than in any other country and less easily borne by virtue of the existing population trends. For every 100 men in the active age groups 10·5 were reported killed or disappeared, a total of 1·3 million. Of those who survived, 1·1 million had suffered war wounds of some sort with over 100,000 wholly incapacitated. The men killed left some 600,000 widows and 750,000 orphans, besides another 900,000 who under the generous French legislation were entitled to some pension from the state.[2]

TABLE 2. *French population (frontiers of 1919)*

	in thousands
1921	39,210
1926	40,744
1931	41,835
1936	41,907

Source: *Annuaire Statistique*, 1966

Civilian casualties due to enemy action were small but mortality from other causes was higher than normal by reason of wartime conditions. The number of births fell drastically compared with what could have normally been expected. Excluding the three departments of Alsace-Lorraine which were restored to France, the total population in 1921 was slightly lower than in 1891. Now, however, it had aged and was to age still further, and it included a

2. Huber, *op. cit.*

significant number of wholly or partly incapacitated men and persons entitled to state pensions. In short, the war intensified a population problem already existing owing to the slow rate of increase registered before the war. It had unfavourable effects on the age composition and the quality of the population and created for employers a general labour scarcity which could only be made good by immigration.[3]

II

The material losses arising from the war are difficult to measure. The first difficulty arises from what should be included and then from whether it is possible to make any quantitative estimate of the loss. First of all there were physical losses attributable to the war: buildings, factories, ships and all other forms of capital destroyed. To this should be added the destruction of forests and natural resources and the land made unfit for cultivation. Secondly, closely connected with the first category, were the stocks used up and the depreciation of capital which took place. Thirdly, a calculation might be made of the production foregone, and thus of the burden borne in terms of real consumption by reason of the turning of the apparatus of production towards the satisfaction of war requirements. In a physical sense the war cost represented the total value of the labour power devoted to the effort of war, and thus to economically unproductive use.

When the financial costs of the war are considered, although it is possible to give figures, the meaning of these figures has to be carefully scrutinised.[4] Some, but not all, of the physical costs were included in the financial balance

---

3. A useful summary of the demographic consequences of the war is to be found in A. Armengaud, *La Population française au XXe siècle,* Paris, 1967, ch. 2. He concludes 'La France avait subi une saignée sans précédent. Sa population, déjà affaiblie par la baisse séculaire de la natalité, se trouvait maintenant amputée d'une forte proportion de ses éléments masculins les plus vigoureux et privée des centaines de milliers d'enfants que la guerre avait empêchés de naître. Sauf réaction rapide, l'avenir même de la population française apparaissait bien plus gravement menacé encore qu'à la veille du conflit' (p. 31).
4. For reparations purposes the French government put the total cost at 34,000 million gold francs. Sauvy adds 10,000 million francs for depreciation, 8,000 million for credits extended to other countries and 3,000 million for the reduction in the Bank of France's gold reserve, *op. cit.,* p. 31.

sheet. When they were they represented payments by the state to individuals and firms which were met either by taxation or by additions to the debt burden. But the 'burden' of debt in turn represents an obligation by the state to a creditor. Unless payments actually had to be made to a foreign creditor, therefore, what was involved was a transfer payment from some individuals or classes to others and not a national impoverishment.

The physical cost of the war thus represented constant capital destroyed or used up in carrying on the war effort, plus lives lost and working capacity impaired, together with the labour time devoted to fighting the war and other military duties and to providing for the needs of the armed forces. Most of this cost had to be borne at the time, leaving to the future the expenses of reconstruction and reconversion and of providing for the incapacitated and the dependents of those killed or wounded.

Debts to other countries incurred by France during the war represented a foreign contribution to the war effort and thus a claim on the future production of the country. A burden was therefore placed on the postwar generation. In the same way, the loss or using up of foreign holdings of French investors or businesses involved the reduction of the national patrimony and of the income which might otherwise have been received from them.

The central difficulty in estimating the cost of the war was one of financial method. Because only about one-sixth of the government's wartime expenditure was met by taxation there was a great increase in the national debt and thus the creation of claims to future income. The huge increase in the national debt was seen in a way analogous to private debt: as a great and terrifying burden. The real problem was twofold. Some sections of society had been enriched in money terms because they had obtained wartime contracts, generally on favourable conditions, which enabled large profits to be made. At the same time, holders of government securities had increased their nominal wealth and now had a lien on future government revenue which had to come from taxation or from more borrowing. In the course of the war an inflationary process had inevitably been unleashed and it was kept stoked up by further government borrowing in the early years of peace, especially for reconstruction purposes. The assumption was, indeed, that the financial costs of the war would be made good by German reparations: that is, by a transfer of commodities and capital from Germany to France. These sanguine hopes were not realised. The country was thus left with an intractable problem of currency inflation which undermined confidence in the franc.

All political and economic problems in the first postwar decade were soon to be overshadowed by the battle for the franc—which was temporarily won by Poincaré's stabilisation in 1926. Attention thus tends to be turned away from other significant changes and trends. But the lack of confidence in the money was in itself an enormous change by comparison with the prewar situation when the stability of the franc had been taken for granted. Now the demand was made for monetary policies which would restore this happy situation, if possible by returning the franc to its prewar gold parity. This turned out to be an impossible goal. Successive governments grappled with the problem of the franc and paid their lip-service to monetary orthodoxy while the demands of practical necessity drove them to financial expedients incompatible with it.

The real significance of the methods used to finance the war and reconstruction was that they redistributed wealth and income flows to the detriment of some families and classes and to the benefit of others. But one of the characteristics of the process was that the gains and losses fell arbitrarily on different families and sections of society. Moreover, gains made in one period might be lost very quickly owing to a change in general business and financial conditions. This was obviously true, for instance, of the peasantry, who gained heavily as a result of the rise in prices during and immediately after the war only to lose when prices of agricultural commodities fell or rose less than other prices in the 'twenties.

To designate the gainers and losers is difficult and efforts made to do so are no doubt subjectively coloured. It seems to be agreed that the larger property owners as a whole conserved or increased their wealth as a result of the war. Industrialists, contractors, merchants—those who controlled production or had goods to sell—did well and accumulated money capital, some making vast new fortunes. They could thus expand their businesses and perhaps buy up or drive out lesser competitors.

IV

Most tears are shed on behalf of 'the middle classes'. The definition of those concerned is generally vague. The economic structure of France fostered the existence of large numbers of small property owners of different degrees of wealth and independence. As a whole the *petite bourgeoisie* was not ruined during or after the war if only because those of its members concerned with the buying and selling of goods did benefit from the wartime prosperity in some fields and from the boom which followed. Even so, many small businesses closed down because their proprietors were mobilised and the ranks of the professional middle classes were disproportionately affected by death and injury at the front. Wartime stringencies and difficulties in obtaining credit must have hit some sections of small business.

It is not easy to say whether middle-class families lost financially during the war and as a result of the postwar inflation unless something is known about the way in which they held their wealth and their source of income. The biggest losers were those who had invested heavily in Russian and other foreign bonds which became worthless. Many prudent small investors before the war had preferred this type of investment as they did also the fixed interest type security issued by public authorities or business firms in France. Such assets depreciated sharply as a result of the inflation. The fate of members of the middle class depended largely on how individual and family savings were distributed between different forms of investment and what activities were carried on. There were possibilities for enrichment as well as for ruin. Though inflation meant hardship for many pensioners, widows and small rentiers after the war, the middle class as a whole suffered less than in Germany and central Europe and was by no means ruined. The undoubted losses experienced by some middle-class people were balanced and outweighed by the gains of others.

The war undoubtedly offered industrialists and war contractors great opportunities for enrichment. Complaints about 'profiteering' and the excessive spending of the *nouveaux riches* were by no means confined to the left wing parties and press. The long-term trend towards the concentration of capital was speeded up as a corollary to the technological changes bred by the war and the rise of new industries. Inflation enabled the big firms to increase their profits while their fixed debt burden was lightened. On the other hand losses were spread through sections of the small and medium-sized bourgeoisie, especially at its lower end among pensioners and small rentiers. Since real estate was a favourite way in which small property-owners held their patrimony, they were affected in time by the fact that rents were kept artificially low by wartime legislation and that land values rose less than other prices. Taken with the disappearance of that landmark of prewar security, a stable franc, it was not surprising that many middle-class people found themselves deprived and disoriented in a world they no longer understood.

Socially, therefore, the war had a cost of its own. It markedly increased the social weight of the industrial proletariat, now more highly organised than before both in trade unions and in political parties. At the same time, many middle-class people, besides seeing their families shattered by bereavement, saw the real value of the paper titles on which their security had depended evaporate or even disappear while they could only watch helplessly. Moreover, while some suffered loss of wealth and a deprecia-tion of status, new arrivals to the ranks of the successful flaunted the wealth acquired by methods and with a speed which caused resentment and threw doubt on the old bourgeois virtues of thrift and enrichment through labour and savings. Numerically speaking more small savers lost through default and inflation than there were industrialists, contractors and speculators who made fortunes. While the upper ranks of the bourgeoisie consolidated their positions large sections of the middle class moved into an era of disillusionment and doubt.

5

RECONSTRUCTION

I

At the end of the war France was confronted with a huge task of reconstructing and repeopling the occupied and devastated regions.[1] In the euphoria of victory it was assumed that the costs would be borne from German reparations. Less apparent was the fact that the war had dislocated the normal channels of international trade and left the one-time second creditor country in the world with a large external debt. The resort to massive borrowing to finance the war had set the franc on an inflationary path, corroding its value on the foreign exchanges and undermining confidence at home. On the other side of the scale may be placed the recovery of Alsace-Lorraine and the acquisition of additional colonies, and the fact that the foundations had been laid for a new surge forward of industrialisation. The war had done a good deal to break up inertia and resistance to change, especially in industry, and to stimulate the adoption of new techniques and forms of organisation.[2]

1. A. Sauvy, *Histoire économique,* i, ch. 11, *passim.*
2. For a detailed description of industrial trends, see W. F. Ogburn, and W. Jaffé, *The Economic Development of Post-War France,* New York, 1929, especially ch. 8.

The first postwar decade was a comparatively brilliant one for French industry. While the difficulties of the franc occupied the centre of the political stage and filled the columns of the press a silent revolution was taking place in some sectors of industry. The compensation payments which swelled the public debt and contributed to inflation had as their counterpart the establishment of a modern industrial complex in the formerly devastated areas, largely reconstructed by 1924. The depreciation of the franc on foreign exchanges gave exporters an advantage from which many were not slow to profit. The weight of fixed debt was also appreciably lightened as inflation continued and costs tended to rise less than prices. Rising prices encouraged spending, and consumption habits were also changing, so that the home market was generally buoyant. To add to the prosperity tourism flourished as foreigners could get more francs for their own currency: investment in resorts, hotels, restaurants and casinos was encouraged. All in all the picture was a dynamic one, favourable to business enterprise and to profits.[3]

II

Why should a country which had suffered so heavily during the war in manpower and in material resources have been able to resume growth so rapidly? More was involved than a brief postwar boom. The French recovery was one example, of course, of the recuperative powers of industrial societies after periods of wartime destruction. Several interconnected factors were involved. Firstly, new possibilities for profitable investment were opened up by the very fact of the destruction or of the running down of equipment during the war. But industry did not have to depend only on its own liquid funds or borrowing to undertake new investment. In the areas of reconstruction these funds largely came from government sources. Inflationary finance had its counterpart, then, in the reconstruction of some of the

3. The combination of boom and inflation is now more familiar than it was then. Ogburn and Jaffé comment with surprise: 'Paradoxically as it may seem, the economic events of postwar France lend themselves to the interpretation that inflation has a stimulating effect on industrial development' (*op. cit.*, pp. 167–8).

country's main industrial areas. At the same time the infrastructure was rebuilt, also with state funds. These large outlays on capital equipment had a variety of linkage effects which encouraged further investment and created more employment and more incomes, thus stimulating consumption goods industries as well.

The main line of development after the war was towards accelerated industrialisation and expansion. It is true that some capacity used for armaments proved to be surplus or could not be reconverted; it is true also that there were some signs of slump felt unevenly in industry between 1919 and 1922. Nevertheless the predominant trend was one of buoyancy and expansion which contained specifically national elements but was supported by a favourable international conjuncture.

The conditions of war and the necessities of reconstruction stimulated industrialisation and modernisation. The tendency in French business to settle down to routine production under fixed conditions for stable markets was for a time rudely shaken. Adaptation to twentieth-century methods was imposed by external conditions and the response, though uneven, was definite enough to bring about a noticeable change in the industrial structure. Important sectors of industry were now rebuilt or re-equipped according to the best world standards where before the war they had often been obsolete and backward. Necessarily this was an uneven process. Only some areas were reconstructed from the ground up; in others ancient equipment continued to operate. The effects of war demand fell more heavily on engineering than on textiles. War and reconstruction had a bigger impact generally on capital goods industries than on consumer goods industries. It could be said even that the contrasts within French industry were sharpened as a result of these changes. On the one hand there were the large-scale, technically advanced, integrated concerns, on the other the small masters and artisans still producing under conditions reminiscent of the eighteenth century. And in between lay a multiplicity of small factories and workshops, typically organised as family firms, still backward in technique, short of capital, and producing a diversity of products at high unit cost.

The destruction of capital during the war and the slow-down in investment opened up new possibilities. The injection of funds from the government in the form of compensation payments, together with the liquid reserves which industry had built up from wartime profits, made possible the financing of new investment. There took place, therefor, a considerable modernisation as well as reconstruction of industrial plant and machinery. In some sectors this meant a complete transformation from prewar obsolescence and inefficiency to the highest technical standards available. As Ogburn and Jaffé put it: 'In a relatively short period, under the influence of powerful stimuli to change, the French industrial equipment, which had been notoriously obsolete, was completely transformed in a great many branches of production and brought up to the highest standards of efficiency.'[4] Speaking of the metallurgical industry, a British observer wrote that during reconstruction 'missions of experts were sent abroad, notably to America, to study the best ore-mining, coke oven, blast furnace, and steel mills practice'.[5]

The building up of capacity in the metallurgical, engineering and chemical industries outstripped the growth of the home market. The general expansion of the 'twenties drew these industries into closer integration with the world market. In a sense the boom of the late 'twenties was exported.[6] The vanguard sectors of French capitalism became more highly dependent on imported raw materials and foreign markets. The economy as a whole, no longer drawing such a large invisible income from foreign investments, was dependent on exports to balance outgoing payments on a greater scale than ever before. Ultimately, therefore, the strength of the franc depended on the competitiveness of French exports. With the onset of the world economic depression the undervaluing of the *franc*

4. Ogburn and Jaffé, *op. cit.*, p. 120.
5. Report by Sir Robert Cahill on *Economic Conditions in France* (Department of Overseas Trade, 1934), p. 214. Earlier he writes: 'Since 1914 the vast majority of iron and steel works within the pre-war frontiers of France have been entirely reconstructed and equipped in the most modern manner, or have been very substantially reorganized and refitted, enlargements having been effected in both cases' (p. 213). The systematic destruction of French industrial equipment in the later stages of the German occupation was reported upon by a series of articles in the financial newspaper *L'Information* during 1920.
6. In 1929 exports reached the highest figure ever.

Poincaré offered at first some protection. Once that had gone the sensitivity of French capitalism to world trends became evident.

Certainly in the 'twenties there were signs of 'a new vigour and aggressiveness in industry'.[7] They were confined mostly to the growth industries which had been pushed out of their grooves by the emergency or which had been rebuilt in the course of reconstruction. Some entrepreneurs pushed ahead in the new, expanding sectors. The big investments made in fixed plant, the scarcity and high costs of fuel and other inputs and the scarcity of labour imposed a drive for greater technical efficiency. The stereotype of the backward, cautious entrepreneur satisfied with a small turnover and high profits does not fit the large-scale, modern sectors in the 'twenties at all accurately.

Needless to say the characteristic weaknesses of French capitalism inherited from the nineteenth century had not been eliminated. Old backward sectors remained which conserved the traditional structures and mentalities. The weight of the agrarian sector had not been drastically reduced. The artisanal and petty commodity production continued to prevail in many industries. Established family firms still persisted and dominated in certain industries, especially textiles. But it was of the metal goods industries that firms were described as 'patrimonial heirlooms cherished by their owners who fondly clung to the rule-of-thumb methods of their fathers'.[8] Persistent contrasts between the most advanced techniques and forms of organisation and the archaic continued to be apparent. The modernising thrust of war and reconstruction had run up against definite limits set by the old structures—by family capitalism, a clinging to routine and a preference for security over risk.

By the time that reconstruction had been completed the

---

7. A phrase used by Ogburn and Jaffé.
8. Ogburn and Jaffé, *op. cit.*, p. 339. They speak of a lack of concentration and co-ordination and 'an incredible diversity of products'.

industrial basis of French capitalism had been considerably strengthened. A shift had taken place towards heavy industry. Industries based on advanced technologies and mechanisation such as chemicals, rayon, electricity, rubber and motor cars had begun to assume a more prominent role. A measure of concentration had taken place in some industries and closer relationships had been established between industry and the banks. The 1920s saw a rapid growth in industrial production and by the end of the de-cade, after Poincaré's stabilisation, the franc had once again become a strong currency. Confidence had been largely restored and a new era of prosperity appeared to have begun.

Industrial employers enjoyed good times during the war and apart from one or two spells of recession did well until the early 'thirties. Money had been made and capital accumulated, debts had been reduced or paid off and plant had been extended and modernised. Apart from the eight-hour day, few concessions had been made to the working class. Trade unionism remained relatively weak in factory industry and the employers' powers and prerogatives were virtually as great as they had been before 1914.[9] In some places they were dealing with a heterogeneous work force including many newcomers from the countryside and immigrant workers. If the employer did not feel disposed to deal with trade unions there was nothing to compel him to do so. In many firms the old paternalism survived with company towns, company housing and company schools and churches. Despite the labour shortage in the economy as a whole employers were able to keep down labour costs at the expense of wages. In the later stages of the boom, indeed, it seems likely that some of the gains in real wages made in the early 1920s disappeared.[10]

9. As C. Fohlen puts it in *La France de l'entre-deux-guerres* Paris, 1966, p. 301, quoting from F. Goguel, *La Politique des partis sous la IIIe République*, i, 217; 'Dans le patronat tout au moins, la guerre a renforcé les idées traditionelles sur les rapports avec les travailleurs. Les patrons "n'ont pas vraiment compris la nécessité de renoncer à certaines de leurs prérogatives pour mettre fin à la lutte des classes. . . . Le patronat s'affermit dans des conceptions rétrogrades. La bourgeoisie méconnaît plus que jamais les facteurs réels du problème social".' The testimony is important coming from authors who retain illusions about putting an end to the class struggle.

10. Lhomme's figures, 'Le pouvoir d'achat . . .', *loc. cit.* (see p. 41, n. 25), suggest that real wages recovered during the price fall of 1921–22, to fall back again in 1926–27. As he puts it, 'il semble bien établi que les ouvriers—toujours ceux qui conservent leur emploi—ont des chances de profiter de la baisse des prix plus qu' ils ne souffrent de la baisse des salaires' (p. 58).

If the bourgeoisie as a class suffered any losses during the war and the postwar inflation, the industrial dynasties must certainly have gained. They did so at the expense, in part, of those on fixed incomes, those who held fixed interest securities. It was the middle-class investing public and small rentiers who followed with anxiety the downward gyrations of the franc until 1926. Meanwhile, however, the industrial basis of French capitalism was being strengthened. The great problem for industry was that of markets, not only the home market but now, more than ever before, the export market. French capitalism as a whole had become much more sensitive to external shocks: this was the price it paid for the modernisation and expansion of the 'twenties.

6

THE BATTLE FOR
THE FRANC

I

The economic history of postwar France, until Poincaré's *de facto* stabilisation of 1926, was dominated by the struggle to save the franc.[1] One unsuspected legacy of the war was the undermining of the monetary unit, which had been artificially maintained first by British and then by American support during the conflict. When this support was removed in 1919 the exchange rate of the franc fell. Until March of that year the dollar rate had been pegged at 5·45 francs. By the end of the year it had risen to about 11 francs and the decline of the franc continued until the end of April 1920, apart from temporary breaks. Following a period of cyclical crisis and industrial depression during which the franc was strengthened it had to face a hostile offensive by speculators which began in November 1923. After the 'battle of the franc' of 1924 there was an interlude of relative calm until, in 1926, the collapse of the franc once

1. Monetary questions gave rise to a mass of literature. Of accessible studies for the student the following works seem particularly useful: (1) the short survey, by A. Neurisse, *Histoire du franc*, 2nd ed, Paris, 1967, (2) the very detailed and competent study by E. L. Dulles, *The French Franc, 1914–1928*, already cited; (3) the interesting and revealing study of the contemporary press, by M. Perrot, *La Monnaie et l'opinion publique en France et en Angleterre 1924–1936* Paris, 1955.

73

again seemed imminent. Poincaré's intervention then put an end to this phase of monetary history and the franc, to all appearances, had become a stable currency.

The reason for the weakness of the franc is to be found in the inflationary methods used to finance the war and the reconstruction which followed it. The expenses of the war were met by increasing the monetary circulation, borrowing from the Bank of France, increasing the long-term debt and issuing short-dated securities known as *bons de la défense Nationale*. The state of French public finances at the time of entry into the war made it difficult to pay for the war in any other way. Further, the demands of reconstruction and the lack of foreign earnings because of the breakdown of the normal trade and payments mechanism left little choice but continued inflationary policies once the war was over.

It was assumed, with a confidence which now seems ridiculous, that 'The Boche will pay', as Klotz, the Finance Minister said. The first postwar years thus saw the illusion of reparations as a solution for France's financial ills first confidently believed in and then quickly smashed. Few people had a realistic grasp of the problems bequeathed by the war and it was generally believed that the restoration of the prewar gold value of the franc would be possible, with the help, of course, of German reparations. Not until 1923, after the entry of French troops into the Ruhr and the collapse of the mark, was it clear that the belief in reparations had been a delusion.

The politicians of the twenties were unable to face up to certain realities or follow through the logic of their actions. The biggest illusion was that the financial cost of the war and of reconstruction could be passed on to Germany. With this belief in mind the government allowed the debt to mount and became dependent on advances from the Bank of France and short-term borrowing from the public. Its account thus became highly sensitive to public confidence, or rather to that section of the public which had monetary reserves and savings. The illusion was also general that it would be possible, despite the fall in the value of the franc which had taken place, to restore prewar parity. For this to have been at all possible a firm stand would have had to be taken against inflation by draconian economy measures.[2]

II

France came out of the war with an inconvertible paper currency and a wholesale price level three and a half times what it had been in 1914. Financial aid from Britain and later from the United States had prevented a big depreciation of the franc on the foreign exchanges, but it fell heavily once that support was removed in March 1919. However, most Frenchmen assumed that the franc would one day resume its prewar gold parity. Postwar monetary history, with its record of inflation and depreciation, was to make this a vain dream. What counted in this period was the value of the franc in terms of the two strong currencies, the dollar and the pound, both of which had depreciated, but to a lesser extent. Until the stabilisation of 1926 the franc was to fluctuate wildly, usually in a downward direction. By then it had fallen to about one tenth of its prewar value.

In fact the situation in 1919–20 was extremely complex. The wartime restraints and controls on prices had been removed and a greatly increased monetary demand began to press on a volume of production which was still much below that of prewar. Generous government financing of the rebuilding and repopulation of the war-stricken territories fed the flames of inflation. War finance, and the expedients of the postwar years, greatly increased the monetary supply of individuals and institutions. Most difficult of all, from the government's point of view, was the dependence upon the *bons de la défense*. Any lack of confidence in the money deterred holders from renewing their lending, thus depriving the government of vital funds and forcing it to look elsewhere, namely to the Bank of France. The decline in the value of the franc in terms of other currencies encouraged the shift of funds into dollars

2. 'Le slogan "L'Allemagne paiera'', qui coincidait au sentiment de la quasi-totalité des Français, servit au Ministre des Finances, Klotz, à justifier une politique de facilité, alors que des mesures draconiennes eussent été indispensables'.—E. Bonnefous, *Histoire politique de la Troisième République*, iii, 23. The problem is why French governments preferred '*une politique de facilité*'?

and pounds and thus aggravated the tendency for the franc to depreciate still further.

A check came to the worldwide postwar boom in the course of 1920. Raw material prices fell, interest rates rose and credit tightened. From June wholesale prices in France began to come down and the movement accelerated during 1921, which was a year of industrial depression, though its incidence was uneven. Stimulated by the continued demands of reconstruction recovery was rapid and industry was booming again in 1922. During the cyclical downturn the franc had made a recovery on the foreign exchanges, while its internal purchasing power also improved. These conjunctural trends were generally interpreted optimistically to signify that further improvement could be expected until the franc would return to its pre-1914 par value. These hopes were soon to be dashed.

During 1922 the reparations crisis began to build up with growing friction between France and her allies concerning Germany's ability to pay and the effect which attempts to exact reparations would have on the recovery prospects of Europe. When the deadlock over reparations became apparent in June the franc came under pressure which was conditioned above all by speculative factors. The occupation of the Ruhr and the spectacular fall in the mark undermined confidence in the franc and brought fears that it would go the same way.[3] In fact the fall in the value of the franc was not accompanied by internal economic difficulties. Production continued to grow and exports benefited from the depreciation of the franc. This lent colour to the view that the franc was the victim of deliberate outside speculation.

From the time that French troops began to march into the Ruhr in January 1923, in an attempt to impose the payment of reparations, the decline in the franc was precipitous. Another fall took place in June, but it was in November and the succeeding months that foreign speculation reached its heights and that the 'battle of the franc' began in earnest.[4] To counter the speculation against the franc the government tried to enhance confidence by

3. Perrot, *op. cit.*
4. The franc stood at 73 to the pound at the end of 1922; at 85 to the pound twelve months later and at 120 at the beginning of March, 1924.

budgetary measures in January and February 1924. Within a few weeks the franc lost nearly half its value and fears grew that it would go the same way as the mark. French capitalists joined with foreigners in a panic flight from a currency which appeared to be on the brink of collapse.

The increases in taxation which it announced enabled the Poincaré government to enlist foreign financial support to resist the speculators. It was able to borrow 100 million dollars from Morgans of New York, and 4 million pounds from Lazards of London. With these funds it stepped into the exchange market as a purchaser of francs, pushed down the sterling and dollar price and outwitted the speculators. Relative stability was once again restored and the franc appreciated by 40 per cent. However, the underlying weakness remained, notably the government's financial difficulties and the large volume of floating debt.[5]

The paradox in this situation is that while parliament, the press and public opinion were preoccupied with a monetary crisis which assumed disastrous proportions, the economy as a whole was prosperous and expanding. As in any inflationary period those who produced goods or had them for sale made more than the anticipated profits. Income tended to be spent more rapidly as confidence in the ability of the franc to conserve its value waned. The depreciation of the franc gave a bonus to exporters in penetrating foreign markets. The expenditures which caused the government so much difficulty meant the growth of some private incomes and the stimulation of business activity. A successful deflation would have put an end to this prosperity and brought new and unknown dangers in its wake. As it was industrial production was steadily catching up with the prewar level and exceeded it by 9 per cent in 1924 and 26 per cent in 1926.

There were, of course, losers from the wartime and postwar inflation: the rentiers, small savers, people on fixed incomes—layers of the middle class who were often inarticulate and powerless. However, the decline in the value of money inflicted hardship on rather than 'ruined' such

5. It was a Pyrrhic victory, according to Neurisse, *op. cit.*, p. 59; 'Le produit des emprunts ne servit qu'à éponger la crise du change et les lourdes échéances de la dette flottante menaçaient à brève échéance la stabilité financière intérieure. L'occasion était une nouvelle fois manquée de consacrer officiellement l'amputation monétaire et de consolider les emprunts à court terme.'

people. What was important was that they were now resentful and felt hard done by; they felt that they had been cheated and that it was all the fault of the politicians. A blow had been struck at the sober bourgeois values of nineteenth-century liberal France. Faith in the stability of the money had been part of the old creed which included the belief in enrichment through work and savings. In a world of inflation and rapid and arbitrary changes in fortune the old certainties no longer applied.

Belief in the desirability of a stable money was so deeply rooted that many of those who in fact benefited from the inflation looked forward to a return to stability and sound finance.

The elections of May 1924 brought to power a coalition of radicals and socialists, the *Cartel des gauches,* under Herriot, to replace the conservative *Bloc national* which had ruled since the end of the war. The shift to the left had been precipatated in part by resentment against the increased taxes. The new government was more amenable than its predecessor to finding a solution to European problems by cooperation with Britain and the USA. The first result, however, was to cause uncertainty in financial circles because of the proposals for a capital levy and other fiscal changes which the victor parties had put forward during the election campaign. These fears were calmed when it was apparent that the *Cartel* was not able to proceed at once with far-reaching changes.

In the course of 1925 a severe confidence crisis began. Fears about the future of the franc had now spread to many small holders of funds who sought refuge in foreign exchange. The government had difficulty in renewing the floating debt as *bons de la défense* fell due and in meeting payment of interest and amortisation on the public debt. It was therefore obliged to depend upon increased advances from the Bank of France as an alternative to repudiation of part of the internal debt. New loans had to be negotiated on unfavourable terms and the note circulation rose. Six finance ministers grappled unsuccessfully with the budgetary problem during 1925 and as public confidence waned so the franc continued to depreciate in an atmosphere of growing panic. At the end of the year the franc stood at 130 to the pound, against 85 twelve months before.

Through a succession of government changes which only added to the crisis of confidence the franc continued to depreciate during the first half of 1926. More people were now alerted to the dangers and acted accordingly. The government found it increasingly difficult to renew its short term borrowings. Withdrawals from the savings banks increased. The main problem continued to be the internal debt and the consequent fear of government insolvency and a collapse of the money. By July the dollar had reached 50 francs and the pound 240. In one year the franc had lost half of its value.

During a brief tenure of the Ministry of Finance M. Raoul Peret had appointed a committee of experts to suggest a plan for the stabilisation of the franc. It reported early in July to his successor, M. Caillaux. It recommended a reduction of government expenditure, a balanced budget, and a foreign loan to deal with capital movements, but not exchange control. By this time public opinion had become increasingly agitated. Foreign tourists and traders were blamed for the fall in the franc and a bus load of Americans was attacked in a Paris street. On 11 July 1926 twenty thousand ex-servicemen demonstrated outside the Chamber of Deputies. These growing signs of panic precipitated the final crisis. An attempt by Herriot to form a government lasted only a few hours. Finally, on 22 July, Poincaré was called upon to form a government of National Union.

IV

The assumption of power by Poincaré at the head of a government of National Union had a reassuring psychological effect on the bourgeoisie and middle-class opinion as a whole.[6] The prospect of currency collapse with all its unknown social consequences seemed to have been definitely avoided. The new premier had advance backing

6. Dulles, *op. cit.*, pp. 195 *seq.*

for whatever measures he thought fit to take and the methods which he used, including a special session of both Chambers at Versailles, were intended to underline their portentous character. Poincaré succeeded with surprising speed. Within a few weeks the franc had ceased to be the major political issue and universal preoccupation as it had been for the previous six years. Stabilisation succeeded; but it did so much more on the basis of a restoration of confidence by political legerdemain than by the discovery or application of new techniques of monetary or fiscal policy.

The operation was simply and strictly one of restoring confidence in the franc and confidence in the ability of the government to meet its commitments. The general economic background was favourable. Industry and trade were prosperous and profits ran high. There was labour scarcity rather than unemployment. If some sections of the middle class had suffered from inflation, much money had been made during and since the war. But the owners of this wealth had lost confidence in the franc and were wary of lending to the government. Instead they bought foreign currency, gold or foreign securities and held their money abroad rather than in France. Restoring confidence meant creating a situation in which French capitalists would repatriate their capital, hold francs and invest in government stock. It was because the moneyed classes found in Poincaré and his team a political combination in which they could have faith that their confidence in the money was restored and stabilisation of the franc became possible.

The political and class aspect of the changes made by Poincaré after becoming premier on 24 July 1926 was more important fundamentally than the fiscal and monetary measures which he began to take. Within a few days a series of tax reforms was made. The advances of the Bank of France to the state were reduced, although in fact this was offset by an increase in the discounting of government paper. The joint session of the Chambers at Versailles established a *caisse de gestion des bons* which set an upper limit to the amount of short-dated securities and separated them from the general treasury account. The proceeds of the tobacco monopoly were put at its disposal, as well as certain other receipts.

These operations raised the question of the desirable parity. No doubt there were many sections of opinion which still looked forward to the day when the franc would return to its prewar parity, the restoration of the *franc germinal*. The vicissitudes of the previous years had made this unrealisable by 1926, though this fact was not always recognised. Poincaré's stabilisation left the franc worth only one-fifth of its prewar parity; it was the franc at *cinq sous*. Even the appreciation of late 1926 was only realised at the price of a deflation which brought symptoms of depression and a rise in unemployment. It was seen, therefore, that any further attempt to raise the value of the franc would require a severe dampening down of domestic activity, higher unemployment and the risk of social discontent. These considerations influenced the rate at which the *de facto* stabilisation took place in December 1926.

The measures announced by the government of National Union were intended more to impress opinion than to provide new technical solutions to the problems of public finance. This they did to perfection. The strain on the franc had relaxed from the moment that Poincaré took office. His government had secured a breathing space. The franc continued to improve on the foreign exchanges and this prepared the way for the *de facto* stabilisation of December 1926 ensured by the intervention of the Bank of France purchasing gold and foreign exchange at a fixed franc price, which brought the pound down to 122·25 francs. As a result the value of the franc fluctuated only within narrow limits and represented approximately one-fifth of its prewar parity. The Bank was able to do this by virtue of the resources now placed at its disposal by its ability to increase the note circulation. With the restoration of confidence, dollars, pounds and gold became available in exchange for francs or, more likely, bank deposits. Within a short time, therefore, the financial position of the Bank of France became extremely strong and the way was clear for full stabilisation of the franc.

Although Poincaré, like most Frenchmen of his class and generation, would have liked to see the franc restored to its prewar parity, he came to the conclusion, or was persuaded by expert advisers, that this was out of the question. After his election victory of April 1929 his position had been further reinforced, and in June a monetary law was introduced which placed the franc on a gold basis for the first time at its existing exchange value. However, the franc was only convertible for ingots in a minimum amount of 215,000 francs, and gold coins were not reintroduced. The stabilisation law thus legalised a state of fact and took advantage of the confidence which the franc at its existing parity enjoyed on the foreign exchanges as well as in France. A long period of monetary agony and uncertainty had been brought to an end by accepting the fact that the franc had been amputated of four-fifths of its value.[7] The stability enjoyed since 1926, the strength of the franc on the foreign exchanges and the new-found prestige of the Bank of France had, by mid-1928, reconciled financial opinion to the inevitable. What seemed to be a solid monetary basis had now been laid for the final phase of postwar prosperity. The conservative victory in the elections of 1928 reinforced the impression that confidence and stability had been restored.

The illusion that reparations payments would solve all France's financial problems was destroyed in the course of 1923. The change of majority in the following year brought a period of governmental instability and no coherent policy. The great financial interests were hostile to the *Cartel des gauches* and had the power to embarrass it seriously. In fact there was not a parliamentary majority either for strong measures against their activities or for a policy of deflation which could gain their confidence. The government drifted from one expedient to another while the franc continued to decline. Finally, when catastrophe seemed imminent, Poincaré reappeared on the scene and, by the impression he gave of meaning business, the current was held and reversed. The battle for the franc had been temporarily won at apparently little cost, but within a short time the onset of the world economic depression was to bring about its resumption, this time under less favourable conditions in France and internationally.

7. According to Jacques Rueff, Poincaré was influenced by Léon Jouhaux who pointed out to him that too high a parity would result in unemployment.—'Sur un point d'histoire: le niveau de la stabilisation Poincaré', *Revue d'économie politique*, lxix, no. 1, 1959.

7

THE INDUSTRIAL BOOM
OF THE 1920s AND
ITS CONTRADICTIONS

I

The keynote of economic change in the 1920s was modernisation and continued industrialisation.[1] In part this was an
extension of the established trends of the pre-1914 years
which had been turning France into a country of advanced
capitalism. The war had intruded into the process by
encouraging the spread of industry to new regions and by
speeding up the adoption of new forms of organisation and
new techniques of production. Reconstruction brought a
wholly new infrastructure and modern, rebuilt plants to the
devastated areas. In addition, France recovered the industrially important areas of Alsace-Lorraine with their steel
mills, textile factories and unique potassium deposits.
Reconstruction, changes in the distribution of income and
in consumption habits, brought about an expansion of the
internal market and encouraged further diversification of
production. In particular, the 'twenties saw the growth of
new 'twentieth-century' industries incorporating advanced

1. W. F. Ogburn and W. Jaffé, *The Economic Development of Post-War France*, ch. 8. In
addition, there is much useful material in R. Cahill, *Economic Conditions in France*,
and in J. Boudet, ed., *Le Monde des affaires en France*, Paris, 1952. A full study of
industrial development in this period has yet to be made; Sauvy does not deal with it
in detail. See C. Fohlen, *La France de l'entre-deux-guerres*, ch. 4 *passim*.

technology—motor vehicles, electricals, aviation, rubber, aluminium and chemicals—and requiring, for the most part, organisation on corporate lines. The establishment of the *franc Poincaré* at the end of the decade, by slightly undervaluing the currency, stimulated an export-led boom to round off the period of postwar prosperity.

The period of expansion in the 'twenties was too short-lived and the transformation of the industrial structure insufficiently profound to remove the weaknesses which the French economy had inherited from the past. At the same time, by gearing the more advanced industries, as well as some traditional ones, more closely to foreign demand it increased the susceptibility of the economy to outside shocks. It proved, therefore, to be particularly vulnerable to the effects of the world economic depression in the following decade. The 'Malthusian' traits which had appeared to be in abeyance during the twenties now came into operation with full force.[2] A period of stagnation began which was to last into the early 1950s.

Of considerable significance in retrospect, despite the growth of the period, was the failure to reduce the weight of agriculture in the economy or to modernise it at a faster rate, together with the slow pace of concentration of industry in many fields and the inefficiency and high cost of the distributive sector, all tending to limit the growth of the internal market. The expansion of the 'twenties concealed but did not remove the causes of retardation which had persisted from the eighteenth century. Once the sources of the expansion had dried up they reasserted themselves; their effect was reinforced by the defensive response which industrialists, financiers and politicians made to the impact of the crisis. What was at issue, in fact, was not merely some wrong policies but a paralysis of will and decision which gripped the ruling class as a whole. The roots of this crisis may be traced back to the war if not further, but it was only in the 'thirties that it manifested itself in full force and in such varied ways.

It is not the intention here to deal in detail with industrial

2. The term is used in the French literature to cover policies designed to limit and restrict production whether promoted by the State or the result of concerted action by interested parties. 'Malthusianism' adjusts supply to demand and produces contraction or stagnation.

history but rather to emphasise what seem to have been the outstanding trends in the interwar period. In particular attention will be drawn to the continued industrialisation which was taking place and the modernisation of substantial sections of industry during the war and in the period of postwar reconstruction. At the same time, while to an increasing extent France was assuming the lineaments of an advanced and modern industrial country, as in the past this remained an uneven process. It was uneven geographically, in that large areas remained primarily agrarian and little touched by modern developments and also between industries. It was uneven over the field of industry as a whole because, while large scale and mass production industries based on the most advanced technological methods assumed a growing weight in the economy, equally characteristic was the continued vitality of artisan industry and the smaller family-type firms whose organisation and even technique remained reminiscent of the previous century.

II

Nothing illustrates more strikingly the restructuring of French industry in the twentieth century than the continued growth of the iron and steel and heavy industries. Their rise can be traced back to the 1880s and had figured prominently in the prewar expansion. The great new steelmaking plants constructed on the Lorraine ore field had been the harbinger of the new-style capitalism of the twentieth century. The scale of production in these plants relative to the size of the market made competition unstable. Outside finance was required on a hitherto unprecedented scale. The iron and steel makers were in any case closely linked together in the famous *Comité des Forges*. The influence of the powerful firms like Schneider-Creusot and de Wendel which dominated the industry was undoubtedly very great.[3] Their prosperity depended, in

3. Schneider was deeply involved in many metal-using industries and had extensive international connections. The big combines had bought up the reconstruction claims of smaller firms and extended their interests in many directions through secret ententes and informal agreements.

any case, upon public contracts in which armaments orders figured largely. It was thus possible to suspect them of exercising an occult influence on the politicians of the day.

The direct effect of the war had been to shatter the old framework of heavy industry which lost a large part of its fuel, raw materials, plant and equipment. From the outset, in August 1914, the government called on the *Comité des Forges* to organise production. Some compensation was obtained for the capacity lost by building new plants and increasing production in the centre and other areas distant from the battle zone. Contracts for steel were also placed with producers in Britain.

After the war the industry confronted an immense task of reconstruction in the occupied and war-devastated zones. In the former the Germans had systematically removed or destroyed most of the plant, which therefore had to be rebuilt from scratch. The finance for reconstruction was largely supplied by generous state compensation payments. These were supplemented by collective or individual loan or bond issues launched on the market in the early twenties. Thus supplied with funds it was possible to rebuild the shattered industry in the north and east on the most modern lines. The tendency was for the rebuilt plants to be on a larger scale than before and for the industry to be more concentrated than hitherto. In any case, the wartime conditions had accustomed industrialists to a greater measure of collective action.

The heavy industries retained certain weaknesses from the past, and this held back their expansion and modernisation before 1914. Old-established family firms, operating in a highly protected market, and one which grew insufficiently rapidly, tended to lag behind technically, to resist amalgamation and to scorn resort to bank or any other kind of outside finance. The movement towards monopoly and concentration had, before the war, been an uneven process. The war, directly by promoting collective action and new methods of production, and through the destruction it wrought, brought about a considerable change in the climate in the iron and steel industry.

Within a few years after the end of the war, not only had wholly new plants arisen in the north and east, but there was also the increased capacity of plants in Normandy and the centre and those acquired in the reannexed part of Lorraine. By 1923 the production of 1913 had been reached and further rapid growth took place in the late 'twenties to reach a peak in 1929.[4] The industry had largely been re-equipped at a high level of technical efficiency. The burden of indebtedness had been lightened by the inflation. Concentration had proceeded much further than before the war. On the surface the picture was one of rapid recovery and brilliant performance.

Prospects for the iron and steel industry were not as bright as they seemed. For one thing the reconstruction of the large scale plants in the east and north and the acquisition of German properties in Lorraine increased the dependence on outside (notably German) supplies of coking coal. This sensitivity had been seen in the early 'twenties and had resulted in the occupation of the Ruhr in 1923. With the growth in production after 1923 a further problem had to be faced—that of markets for growing output. During the period of reconstruction the rebuilding of infrastructure and the re-equipping of industry had provided a major outlet. After that home demand grew more slowly—it reflected the weakness of the French economy as a whole—and the industry came to be dependent on an increasing volume of exports. In short, it was forced into the world market.

The prosperity of the industry, assisted by the under-valuation of the franc, thus became tied to the international conjuncture and, as far as coal supplies were concerned, to

4. *Pig iron production* (thousands of tons)   *Steel ingots and castings*

1913	5207 (prewar territory)	4687
1920	3434	3050
1921	3417	3102
1922	5229	4534
1923	5432	5110
1924	7693	6900
1925	8494	7446
1926	9432	8430
1927	9273	8306
1928	9981	9500
1929	10364	9711
1930	10035	9447

Source: I. Svennilson, *Growth and Stagnation in the European Economy,* Geneva, 1954, pp. 258, 262.

political relations with Germany. In the late twenties it benefited from the worldwide boom and from the inelasticity of steel supply in other countries. To a certain extent, therefore, the industry boomed by filling the gaps in the home production of other countries or as a result of the high level of capital investment internationally. High profits were undoubtedly made in these years. However, technical change continued to be rapid and foreign competition was keen. The industry could only retain the advantages derived from the earlier period of reconstruction by continuous modernisation and by heavy and increasingly costly expenditures on new plant and equipment.[5] Everything depended on the maintenance of boom conditions and a high level of foreign demand.

French industrialisation had always been handicapped by the inadequacy of the coal resources of the country, especially the lack of good coking coal. Despite the expansion of production in the Pas de Calais and the development of modern large-scale pits in the latter part of the nineteenth century demand always remained well ahead of home supply. The coal industry was struck a savage blow by the war but, as in the case of the steel industry, the tasks of reconstruction were undertaken rapidly and energetically. Within a few years the mines had been reopened on the most modern lines.

As in the case of iron and steel, reconstruction of the coal mining industry was financed largely by the state, but the northern collieries also joined together to float two public loans in 1921 and 1922. In the course of reconstruction a number of fusions took place and there was a general process of concentration and rationalisation all through the 'twenties. By the middle of the decade the prewar output had been attained and the rise in output continued until the depression set in. Because of the overall national demand

5. Eugène Schneider put it as follows: 'Les installations exécutées à grand frais vieillissent rapidement, un outillage récent peut être mis demain en état d'infériorité par un rival né d'hier.' Quoted in Boudet, *op. cit.*, p. 113.

for coal the industry had no problem in finding outlets for all it could produce until then. Although there were some large combines, as well as mines which formed part of metallurgical concerns, cartellisation had not appeared. However, the mineowners had become accustomed to collective action through the *Comité Central des Houillères de France,* a 'peak organisation' similar to that of the *Comité des Forges.*[6]

French heavy industry, with steel at its centre, was especially hard hit by the depression which struck in the early thirties, for reasons which should now be clear. Once the market contracted and profits fell it became virtually impossible to amortise past investments and difficult to raise fresh capital. A pessimistic reassessment of prospects in a period of financial instability and growing social and political uncertainty brought all the restrictive effects of monopolisation into play. The industry used its control over output to keep up prices by cutting back on production and tried to reinsure itself against the effects of the depression by measures which helped to intensify it for the rest of the economy.

As a result, not only did production fall catastrophically but recovery became more difficult. Without continuous investment in modernisation and in keeping pace with new technological advances the industry was bound to fall behind and became outclassed in international competition. Moreover, the position was aggravated by the fact that after 1931 the franc had become an overvalued currency. This priced French products out of many markets and confirmed the pessimistic and restrictionist trends which had begun to take hold of heavy industry. The whole economy became snarled up in a vicious circle and the stagnation of the 'thirties provided an outstanding contrast with the brilliant performance of the previous decade.

IV

Other sectors of large-scale industry followed a pattern broadly similar to that of iron and steel. Stimulated by the war, in the unoccupied areas, reinvigorated by the large

6. Cahill, *op. cit.,* p. 135.

scale investments of the reconstruction period, they soared through the 'twenties on a wave of expansion. For example, profound changes took place in the chemical industry, both in heavy chemicals and in synthetics. Much new plant was built, also on a large scale and generally according to the best techniques available. This rapid growth was accompanied by a high degree of concentration so that the industry was dominated by a few giant tentacular firms. The French synthetic dyestuffs industry, dominated by Kuhlmann, assumed fourth place in the world. This firm was steadily absorbing independents throughout the 'twenties and 'thirties. St-Gobain, which dominated the plate glass field and had a strong place in industrial and agricultural chemicals, followed a similar path.

Chemicals were typical of the new 'dynamic' sectors of French industry which depended on the application of advanced chemical or physical processes and on the technological discoveries of the late nineteenth and twentieth centuries. Most of the new industries were represented in France either because of the activities of French entrepreneurs or because of the entry into the protected market of foreign branch firms.[7] While factories were often built in the existing centres of industrial concentration—in the north, the centre and in the Paris industrial belt—other plants, by their nature, went to new locations. This was obviously so in the case of the electrochemical and electrometallurgical industries, which manifested a strong thrust forward during and after the war. These industries, such as aluminium, consumed vast amounts of electric power and thus gave a strong stimulus to the development of France's water-power resources, *la houille blanche*; this was especially welcome in view of the continuing shortage of coal supplies and the new and growing dependence on imported petroleum.

A powerful development also took place in the motor car industry and the other industries connected with it. A number of French firms, Renault, Panhard and Peugeot,

7. While the establishment of German branch plants in France had caused some concern before 1914, the new invasion, though on a much more modest scale than after the Second World War, was mainly American.

had already built up a strong position before 1914.[8] They benefited from war contracts, adopted assembly line methods and geared themselves to the growing middle-class market for private vehicles. They were joined by the brilliant entrepreneur, André Citroën, who had made his fortune producing shells during the war. There were also a number of specialised commercial vehicle builders and large accessory manufacturers, notably the tyre firm of Michelin. A notable associated development was the building of big oil refineries by the international petroleum firms as well as by French interests.

V

Turning to the more traditional consumer goods industries, the predominant impression is that the old-style family capitalism had been largely preserved and not even basic-ally changed by reconstruction. These industries were also the strongholds of even smaller petty commodity or artisan production carried on in small workshops or back rooms. Their continued heavy weight in the economy contributed to the special characteristics of French capitalism, to traits conserved from the previous century or even earlier. It was here that the often repeated strictures on French entre-preneurship can be shown to be most valid. Change was slow and much which was archaic in techniques of produc-tion, in organisation and in methods of marketing was preserved.

Part of this sluggishness and addiction to routine can perhaps be explained by the slow growth of the home market, a reflection of the continued weight of the low-income peasant or artisan households and of the unfavour-able demographic trends. But many of these industries also had a place in the export trade. Here they held their position not on cost but on quality and finish, on their ability to follow the vagaries of fashion or changes in demand, espe-cially as far as those connected with the dress trade were concerned. It is understandable, therefore, that such

8. Until 1929, with a production of 245,610 vehicles, France was the largest producer in Europe, losing that place to Great Britain in the following year.

industries were resistant to large-scale production and mechanisation. They depended upon specialised, skilled and at the same time low-paid labour.

Textiles made up a large part of the traditional sector of capitalist industry. The character and location of these industries had been determined back in the nineteenth century or even earlier. Even the larger firms were still essentially family concerns and, while they might, for legal convenience, assume the joint stock form, control and finance remained with the heirs of the founders. French entrepreneurs, confronted by a powerful rival in the nineteenth century, had sought lines of production in which they had, or could acquire, an advantage which he did not have. Thus, since the world market in cheap cottons was dominated by Lancashire, the producers in Normandy or northern France depended mainly on the home market. On the other hand, in higher quality lines, in worsted yarns and dress fabrics, or in fancy goods, a strongly competitive position in the high-income markets of the world had been established.

Most striking of all was the performance of the silk industry which enjoyed thirty years of unbroken prosperity until the depression of the 'thirties. Rising incomes in the advanced countries, a strong position built up over centuries, high levels of design and quality and an unrivalled reputation were the foundations of its success. It was centred on Lyons and had only scattered outposts in the war-scarred territories. It thus continued to prosper during the war and was strongly placed to take advantage of the boom which followed it. But it did so without major technical or organisational change. Most silk mills were on a small scale, family-run concerns, while in the weaving branch there were hundreds of separate firms and organisation was still, for the most part, at an artisan stage. Nevertheless 70 per cent of output was exported at the end of the 'twenties and it remained the leading export industry.

However, clouds were already hanging over the silk industry. The competition of rayon had begun to become serious and although the industry could and to some extent did adapt itself to the new fibre foreign competition was bound to become more acute. Cheap factory-made goods having the appearance and some of the qualities of silk began to flood on to the market. Further, the silk industry, like other export trades, had been favoured by the under-valuation of the franc and it was hard hit by the unwilling-ness of the French government to devalue after 1931. This aggravated the effects of the world economic depression which cut luxury spending and also curtailed the flow of tourists into France who bought silk goods and other French specialities during their stay.

The depression thus had a devastating effect on the textile industries, especially those whose prosperity dep-ended on export trade. In all exports of textiles fell by some 80 per cent between 1929 and 1932.[9] On the face of it there should have been a fundamental transformation to meet the crisis, but the inherited structure made this difficult. The family firms could retrench and survive. The artisans could accept a cut in income. The industry was too fragmented to make control over output and price easy. There was a process of adaptation but it was slow. Some larger groups emerged able to rationalise production and turn towards the mass market but the conditions for concentration were much less mature than in heavy industry. Much of the burden was thus thrown on the workers in the shape of unemployment, short time and low wages. There was little trade union organisation until 1936 and it fell back again in the reflux which followed the strikes of that year.

VI

The needs of war industry had added thousands of new recruits to the wage-earning class. An industrial proletariat was created in many places from the peasantry where one

9. The following figures of texture exports (in millions of francs) illustrate the scale of the disaster:

	Cotton	Silk and rayon	Woollens	Clothing
1928	2,963	3,819	2,339	2,096
1929	2,713	3,429	2,095	1,844
1930	2,145	2,866	1,571	1,662
1931	1,414	1,989	1,099	691
1932	971	1,083	419	192

Source: Cahill, *op. cit.,* App. 11, pp. 701–2.

had not existed before. Many women joined the ranks of the factory workers. The size of the peasantry, its continued weight in the total population, made it a continuous source of recruitment and the relatively high wages which prevailed in wartime assisted the movement. But still it had its limits. Agriculture was also short of hands and in the general penury peasant incomes rose to unprecedented heights. The fact that many peasants owned their holdings, or had the chance of acquiring one by inheritance or marriage, as leaseholders or share-croppers, had always acted as a brake on the rural exodus and it continued to do so after the war. The agrarian population suffered disproportionately from the slaughter in the trenches. While some of the survivors evidently felt the attractions of town life, others returned to vacant holdings or felt obliged to fill the gaps which the war had torn in the peasant family.

In any case recruitment from the peasantry alone was quite inadequate to meet the needs of French capitalism during the fresh expansive wave which it entered after the war. It was, indeed, beset by an all-round labour scarcity unusual and exceptional in an old, advanced capitalist country—a product of the demographic stagnation of the pre-1914 period. The problem had been aggravated by wartime loss of life and by the physical incapacitation of many of the survivors, but it had its roots much further back. It was the combination of a peasant economy based on family ownership and partible inheritance with the limitation of births in the peasantry and, by the late nineteenth century, the working class as well, which brought an almost stagnant total population and a continuing low birth rate. France thus become a country of large-scale immigration of foreign workers, such as Poles to the northern coalmines and factories had already begun before the war. Further immigration had been encouraged by the government to meet the needs of war industry and this policy continued after the war. Large draughts of foreign manpower were required to carry through reconstruction and to man the rebuilt and growing industries of the 1920s.[10]

10. Italians formed the largest single contingent, with well over 800,000 estimated to be resident in France in December 1931; Belgians, Polish and Spanish workers made

The mines of northern France and the rebuilt steel mills of Lorraine both relied heavily on immigrant workers. The total numbered over three million by the end of the decade. Many were in large-scale factory industry and the mines, others went into building and construction or wherever wages could be earned. French capitalism thus found at its disposal a mobile labour force which could be drawn quickly to where it was most needed. Unorganised, not speaking the language, unfamiliar with the habits of the country, such workers could be rapidly geared to the needs of industry and made to work intensively for low wages.

For the French proletariat unemployment was not a serious problem until the depression and even then the risks were smaller than in Germany, Britain or the United States. The stagnation in population growth and the peculiar features of the French industrial structure saved it from this scourge to a greater extent than in other countries. Despite what appears to be an overall scarcity of labour power, however, wages did not reflect this as much as might have been expected. The presence of a large proportion of immigrant workers in large-scale industry, such as the Lorraine steel works, was partly responsible. Also there was the fact that French trade unionism, precisely in factory industry, was at this time still weak; the power of the *patronat* was correspondingly unchallenged. Some employers even claimed to be surprised and shocked when the low wages paid to workers in their own plants were pointed out to them during the strikes of 1936.

The fact is that there was not a homogeneous labour market but a series of very imperfect markets and that, despite the appearance of an all-round labour scarcity, circumstances favoured the employers. They took advantage, of course, of the lack of union organisation and of the heterogeneity of the labour supply. They were able to play one section off against another and, in many cases, to call on a ready supply of new, raw immigrants. But in many

---

up the next three largest groups. Many were, of course, seasonal workers or did not intend to make their home permanently in France. In the 'twenties an elaborate government organisation to recruit foreign workers was in being but with the onset of the depression regulations made it impossible for a foreign worker to enter the country without a labour contract approved by the government. See, for example, Cahill, *op. cit.*, pp. 29–34.

towns, in the textile areas for example, conditions in the market also favoured the employers by virtue of their monopsonistic position as purchasers of labour power. Generally a reservoir of labour power also existed in the countryside. There were 'peasant-workers' not wholly dependent upon wages for their means of existence but who were also immobile because of their attachment to their holdings. There were large numbers of underemployed or partly employed people in the rural and semirural areas. Rarely were the workers in a strong bargaining position unless or until they had the backing of a trade union with some pretension to regional if not national coverage of the grade of labour involved.

The paradox of a weak bargaining position and low wage levels in a general environment of labour scarcity and little unemployment can thus be explained along these lines. Without a recognition of this situation, unfavourable as far as the working class is concerned, it is difficult to understand the significance of the strikes of 1936 and the change which was wrought in industrial relations as a result. By this time the new recruits to the proletariat of the war and postwar periods had become more fully incorporated into the class and were no longer prepared to accept the prevailing levels of wages and working conditions.[11] The economic expansion of the twenties, through its effect on the working class, thus prepared the way for the events of May and June 1936.

VII

The industrial upsurge of the twenties resulted from a combination of factors which disappeared in the next decade and confronted French entrepreneurs with a wholly

11. Leon Trotsky had pointed this out in 1929 in writing about the effect of the economic expansion on the working class movement: 'Il faut dire tout net que, pour la class ouvrière française qui, à deux reprises au moins, a renouvelé sa composition sociale: pendant la guerre et après la guerre, qui, de la sorte, a incorporé dans ses rangs d'immenses quantités de jeunes, de femmes, d'étrangers, et qui est loin d'avoir fondu cette substance humaine dans sa cuve, pour la classe ouvrière française, l'évolution ultérieure de l'essor industriel, créerait, une école incomparable, cimenterait ses rangs, montrerait à ses couches les plus arriérées leur importance et leur rôle dans le mécanisme capitaliste et, en conséquence, porterait à un plus haut niveau la conscience que la classe ouvrière a d'elle-meme. Deux ou trois ans, voire une année de

new and intractable situation. Industry had been swung into the boom by generous reconstruction payments. The state had re-equipped large sectors of French industry on modern lines and made it more competitive in world markets than it had ever been before. The decline of the franc to which this largesse contributed benefited industry in other ways—by lightening the burden of fixed debt charges and by stimulating exports. The rise in world incomes during the international boom of the 'twenties enabled French exporters to boost their sales to unprecedented levels. By the end of the decade, therefore, an export-led boom had taken over from reconstruction and the home market in feeding the expansion.

These favourable conditions were, however, to be short-lived. If the crisis struck France belatedly, chiefly because of the undervaluation of the *franc Poincaré*, when it did so, after the sterling crisis of the autumn of 1931, its effects were all the more severe. The franc became overvalued and French goods were now priced out of many markets at the very time when incomes had been cut and competition had become sharper.

The high profits on which industrialists had depended to finance continued re-equipment and modernisation were now threatened. They fell back on the traditional defensive response—a demand for a protected home market and restriction of output to maintain price. As a solution it did not work; in fact it aggravated the difficulties, which were rendered still more acute by a government financial policy imprisoned in orthodox canons which sought to impose deflation as a solution to the crisis. The home market also contracted or ceased to grow at the pre-crisis rate. People held more banknotes and idle balances, assuming that prices would go down still further. Uncertainty about the future cut investment and spending, especially by the middle class.

The typical response of industrialists to the depression thus tended to make recovery more difficult. The same can

---

lutte économique large et victorieuse transfigureraient le prolétariat. Et, après une juste utilisation de l'essor économique, la crise de conjoncture peut donner une sérieuse impulsion à une réelle radicalisation politique des masses.'—'Crise de conjoncture et crise révolutionnaire du capitalisme' (22 decembre 1929) in P. Bronué, ed., *Le Mouvement Communiste en France*, Paris, 1967, p. 308.

be said of the policy of the governments which succeeded each other until 1936 with their strict adherence to the *franc Poincaré* and the principle of budgetary equilibrium. Similar strictures can be applied to the behaviour of consumers. What has to be explained is more in the nature of a general paralysis of will which afflicted the ruling class. More specifically there is the economic problem of why the French economy showed only weak signs of recovery from 1934 onwards when most other capitalist countries had begun to climb out of the trough. Why was there no powerful force making for recovery? Government policy, 'Malthusianism' (i.e. the restriction of output), the overvaluation of the franc, the reasons why housing sagged and 'new' industries failed to provide a lifeline—they must all enter into any reasoned explanation of the failure of French capitalism in the 'thirties. Before returning to this problem it is necessary to examine some other aspects of the decade and the attempt made, in the 'Blum experiment', to grapple with the problem.

8

THE IMPACT OF
THE DEPRESSION 1931–36

I

If the onset of the world economic depression be dated from the Wall Street crash, the signs of its impact in France were scarcely visible for another two years.[1] When they did appear they sharply reversed the trends of the 'twenties and inaugurated a period of decline and stagnation which, complicated by the Second World War and its aftermath, lasted until the mid-1950s.[2] While other countries began their recovery in 1933 or 1934 there was no upturn in France until the latter part of 1935. It was checked by the effects of the Popular Front victory of May 1936, and by the social measures it was obliged to take to satisfy the claims of the working class. Despite the stimulus of rearmament in the last prewar years recovery remained incomplete on the outbreak of the war. There had been no revival comparable with that in the other industrial countries.

1. For an impression of France as a 'slump-proof nation' see *Slump! A Study of Stricken Europe Today*, London, 1932, by the journalist H. H. Tiltman, 'I left the country', he writes 'without having met a single man, employer or official, worker or workless, who was seriously perturbed by the crisis. Which is a remarkable fact. Perhaps God is a Frenchman after all', p. 238. But France was ceasing to be 'a happy island' even before his departure.
2. A. Sauvy, 'The economic crisis of the 1930s in France', in *Journal of Contemporary History*, iv, n. 4, 1969.

The initial period of immunity can be explained mainly from the fact that the franc remained undervalued.[3] The export-led boom of the late 'twenties was thus prolonged in a milder form, despite the falling off in world trade, as long as export prices enjoyed a competitive edge and tourists still found France a cheap place in which to spend a holiday. The real turning point therefore came with the devaluation of the pound sterling in September 1931, which heralded a round of competitive exchange depreciation from which France held aloof for half a decade. During that time the maintenance of the *franc Poincaré* priced many French exports out of the world market and, together with falling incomes everywhere, inflicted a severe blow to the tourist industry.[4] The governments which succeeded each other after 1931, together with the monetary authorities and most expert opinion, considered that first priority should be given to the maintenance of the gold value of the franc. This required a sustained effort to compress the price and income structure and inflicted on the economy the pro-longed agonies of deflation just at the time when all the forces of the market were working towards depression. These years therefore witnessed the last sustained attempt to impose deflation as a remedy for depression. The effect was almost fatal; only the impossibility of carrying out a deflationary policy to the full prevented economic break-down. As it was, deflation contributed to the rising tide of discontent in the working and middle classes, expressed in the victory of the Popular Front and the great strike wave which followed hard on its election.

Although devaluation would have assisted recovery both directly and by giving the government room for carrying out antidepression measures, it is hardly likely it would have been enough to insulate French capitalism from a crisis which was world wide. Furthermore, there were certain factors in internal development contributing to and aggravating the situation. These made the effects of the depression in France, and more particularly the response

3. T. Kemp, 'The French economy under the *franc Poincaré*', in *The Economic History Review*, second series, xxiv, no. 1, 1971.
4. Receipts from tourism are estimated to have fallen from 8·5 hundred million francs in 1930 to 2·5 hundred million in 1932 according to L. Rist and R. Schwob in *Revue d'économie politique* liii, 1939, p. 539.

to it of the government, different from that in other countries.

II

The increased dependence of French capitalism on the world market was demonstrated by the dramatic decline in exports and tourism. This was the principal initiating source of the sharp fall in output in the main export industries, and especially in silk and other textiles, leather and the luxury trades, recorded after 1931. In that year there was a significant fall already in total industrial production. The downward trend continued through the following year with a slight recovery in 1933. Then, no doubt partly as a result of the devaluation of the dollar, there were further falls in the next two years. There were signs that the fall was too great to be attributable to the overvaluation of the franc alone. In 1934 *The Economist* remarked: 'French exports are beaten everywhere, not only by the countries off the gold standard, but actually by other gold countries.'[5] The collapse of exports, for that is what it amounted to, and their failure to show signs of recovery, suggests cost rigidities and a falling off in competitiveness in crucial sectors of industry, old and 'new', whether highly concentrated or still organised on a family basis.[6] Are there some peculiarly French conditions which can explain the failure of industry to respond to the situation in a more aggressive way?

The response of businessmen has to be seen in relation to the worsening social crisis which accompanied the economic depression. True there had been outstanding entrepreneurs who had seized the possibilities offered by the buoyancy of the 'twenties and who give the lie to the stereotype of the French businessman as hidebound by tradition and routine.[7] But there were strong forces of social conservatism to be found in business circles as well as in the bourgeoisie as a whole. The tremors of the war were still

5. *The Economist*, 21 August 1934, p. 871.
6. There were fears also that the loss of overseas markets was permanent owing to the spread of industrialism and to changes in consumption habits away from the type of goods in which French industry had excelled.
7. Fohlen, *La France de l'entre-deux-guerres*, p. 71.

being felt. The depreciation of the franc had undermined security. Neither the uncertainties of the international situation, nor the growing strength of the working-class movement at home did anything to increase confidence in the future. The psychosis of boom was built on fragile foundations; the good years hardly lasted long enough to effect a permanent change in habits of outlook. When the depression began it was seen immediately as constituting a threat to the newly stabilised franc. The maintenance of the *franc Poincaré*, fear of a further catastrophic slide in the value of money, an addiction to balanced budgets—these concerns were uppermost. Basically they reflected a deep-seated crisis of confidence in bourgeois France.

In these circumstances governments were committed to a policy of deflation as the only way to save the franc. The attempt to cut public expenditure and produce a balanced budget or even a budget surplus, so far as it was successful, not only made it impossible to counteract the depressive trends which rapidly flowed through the economy after the devaluation of the pound, it positively assisted them. At the same time, the right of capital-owners to move their holdings, including gold, to foreign centres, was regarded as imprescriptable—even by the government of the Popular Front—so that there could be no question of resort to exchange control. Financial policy was thus rigidly orthodox. No breaches had yet been made in the classical dogmas of economic liberalism, at least in theory. In practice, as prices broke and incomes declined, as farmers, shopkeepers, merchants and industrialists faced bankruptcy, the state began, on an empirical basis, to build up a complex and inchoate array of interventionist measures which interfered with the free operation of market forces in order to preserve certain *situations acquises*.

It is difficult to know what interests determined the parity decided on for the franc stabilisation of 1928, or to explain exactly why there was such determined resistance to changing it in the following years.[8] Many observers,

8. Bouvier's observation is valid for this as for other questions of economic policy in the interwar period: 'Que savons-nous du pouvoir *économique* de la bourgeoisie d'entreprise et d'affaires? du grand négoce? de la grande banque? Qu'en savons-nous surtout entre les années 1880 et 1930? Un demi-siècle de croissance capitaliste et de pouvoir effectif de la grande bourgeoisie échappe, dans une mesure considérable, à

including the correspondents of *The Economist*, were in no doubt that unwillingness to countenance devaluation hindered recovery.[9] In France the case for devaluation did not begin to receive much public expression until about 1934. Even then Paul Reynaud was virtually the only prominent politician to espouse devaluation publicly; the reception he received, in parliament as well as from the press and public opinion, did little to encourage others to follow his example.[10] The experience of inflation and depreciation in the 'twenties had had a traumatic effect on the French rentier, who yearned for the monetary stability of the *franc germinal* which the war had undermined for good. No single important organ of the press supported Reynaud, and a solid bloc, from the Regents of the Bank of France to the Central Committee of the Communist Party, demanded that the 1928 Parity should be maintained.

The opposition to devaluation in all sections of the bourgeoisie between 1931 and 1936 exceeded all rational limits.[11] It was not simply that the virtues of the gold standard had become a dogma and that the effects of devaluation, its advantages and disadvantages, were seldom discussed coldly and dispassionately in the press and other organs of public opinion. There was, undoubtedly, unbelievable ignorance of economic questions in business as well as political circles.[12] Organisations representing exporters, for example, those most likely to benefit by a devaluation of the franc, were among those which went strongly on record against it, though without giving any

---

nos investigations. Il semble que dans l'historiographie française sociale contemporaine, nous avancions bien plus vite dans la connaissance des classes dirigées que dans la connaissance de la classe dirigeante. C'est une constatation qui me paraît même s'aiguiser à mesure que le temps s'écoule." J. Bouvier, *Histoire économique et histoire sociale*, Geneva, 1968, p. 34.

9. It was more obvious to outsiders than to Frenchmen that the crisis could not be tackled as long as the disparity between French and world prices had not been removed by devaluation of the franc. See, for example, reports in *The Economist*, 'France in the depression', 11 August 1934; 'France's economic problem', 27 April, 1935; 'France and the franc', 21 December, 1935.

10. See the accounts of abusive letters received recorded in his autobiography, *Mémoires: Venu de ma montagne*, i, Paris, 1960, vol. i.

11. Perrot, *La Monnaie et l'opinion publique* . . ., p. 221 *seq.* gives many quotations from the general and financial press. Organs of the *patronat* blamed the social legislation passed since 1918 for the troubles of industry.

12. À point insisted upon by Sauvy, *Histoire économique*, ii.

clear economic reasons.[13] Such a lack even of a knowledge
of where self-interest stood, as well as an inability to
consider devaluation as a technical matter to be considered
on its merits, can only be explained in the light of the deep
crisis of confidence, amounting to fear and panic, which
seized the bourgeoisie as soon as the economic crisis began
to grip France. All the fears of social revolution which had
been latent during the 'twenties now rose to the surface. But
whereas in some countries, perhaps because economically
the situation was more desperate, the ruling class turned
to authoritarian methods of rule which at least offered a clear
and determined policy, in France there was division,
hesitation and a sheer paralysis of will. The growth of the
working class as an organised political force seemed to
bring the revolution nearer. But a sound money was
considered to be one of the foundations of the social order.
Strange as it may seem, many responsible leaders and
spokesmen for the bourgeoisie believed that devaluation
would open the floodgates through which the proletarian
hordes would pour. Defence of property was identified with
defence of money. To suggest tampering with it, if not
actually subversive of the social order, prepared the way for
those who sought its overturn.

From 1932 the economy began to display all the symptoms of deceleration and then plunged into the trough of
the depression. The immunity ended suddenly and un-
expectedly. While the 'sheltered' industries mainly serving
the home market were only mildly affected, the export
industries entered on a catastrophic decline. This symbolised France's growing interdependence with the world
market which had accompanied industrialisation. However,
the export industries, although they had led the way in the
closing stages of the boom, did not have the same weight as
in some other countries. Overall the economy was less
export-oriented than that of Britain or Germany. Some
industries which in these countries were extremely hard hit
by the collapse of world trade were less heavily represented
in France. For example, shipbuilding, though doing badly,

13. In 1935, of 1156 Chambers of Commerce and similar bodies concerned with
foreign trade which replied to an enquiry made by the Comité National des Conseillers
du Commerce Extérieur, only 10 were favourable to devaluation, Perrot, *op. cit.*,
p. 228.

was on too small a scale to affect the demand for steel, machinery and products of other industries. Likewise, although the coal-mining industry did feel some effects from the depression, since it supplied only part of the home market in the best of times, and was not an export industry, it did not experience the calamitous decline which afflicted it elsewhere. The same was true of the textile industry to a certain extent. French industry had never had a strong export position in cottons and cheap textiles in the Far East and other areas where Japanese and Indian competition became intense. On the other hand, the Lyons silk industry, the leading export industry which had prospered enormously since the war, slumped heavily as incomes fell, competition intensified and consumers shifted to cheaper substitutes. The industrial impact of the depression was thus unequally spread; in the case of the worst hit production fell not only below that of 1929 but below that of 1913 as well. There could be no doubt about the severity of the industrial slump.

While the government concentrated on deflation and restriction, peasants, artisans and industrial firms sought to defend themselves from the effects of overproduction and falling prices in the same spirit. Protective duties were increased and reinforced with quotas and other administrative devices to keep out foreign goods. But the slump was not confined to foreign demand; the home market also contracted or stagnated and prices continued to fall. Producers who were strongly organised and firms which enjoyed a monopolistic position in the market curtailed production in an effort to maintain prices and profits, heedless of the contractionist effects elsewhere. Those who operated under competitive conditions sought government support in curtailing production, limiting competition and generally shielding them from the operation of competitive forces. The effect was the same. The 'Malthusian' policy of tailoring supply to demand, as it spread from one sector to another, had an all-round decelerating effect. Production continued to fall and even when it showed some signs of rising again the upturn was not sustained.

Although the home market was increasingly protected and insulated as far as possible from the world market this did nothing to ensure recovery and may have had the reverse effect. When other countries began to recover the depression in France continued: there was no home market recovery either. Studies of the 'thirties in Britain have pointed to the rise of 'new' industries and the expansion of house-building as two of the major components in recovery.[14] Neither of these factors operated in France. While in the 'twenties 'new' industries such as motor cars and chemicals had gone through a phase of expansion and had assumed quite a strong international position, they showed no sign of being able to lift the economy out of the trough. For example, motor vehicle production fell back from a peak in 1929 to a trough in 1932; despite a slight recovery in the following two years production in 1935 was scarcely above the 1932 level and the rise in production in the following years remained unimpressive. In Britain the picture is much more like stagnation at little below the 1929 level with a sustained recovery from 1933; by 1936 output was nearly twice as high as in 1929.[15] The pattern was repeated in associated fields and in other 'new' industries. In housing, pre-eminently a 'sheltered' industry, the fall back from the 1930 level to the end of the decade was uninterrupted.[16] Housebuilding virtually ground to a halt. The standard of maintenance and repair fell. These dis-

---

14. e.g. 'The basis of economic recovery in the 1930s: a review and a new interpretation', ch. 7 of D. H. Aldcroft and H. W. Richardson, *The British Economy, 1870–1939*, London, 1969,
15. The following comparative table of motor vehicle production is instructive:
Motor vehicles 000's

	France	UK		France	UK
1926	192	198	1932	163	233
1927	191	212	1933	189	286
1928	223	212	1934	181	343
1929	253	239	1935	165	404
1930	230	237	1936	204	462
1931	201	226	1937	201	508

Source: Ingvar Svennilson, *Growth and Stagnation in the European Economy*, Geneva, 1954, Table 40, p. 149.
As will be seen, while British production more than doubled between 1929 and 1938, French production did not recover before the war. Production of commercial vehicles sagged badly, reflecting the fall in business investment. Tractor production remained puny, especially considering the size of the agrarian sector.
16. *France: New Dwellings (000's)*

1926	1927	1928	1929	1930	1931	1932	1933	1934	1935	1936	1937	1938
110	80	111	122	199	145	138	117	119	116	86	73	67

appointing results must therefore be explained largely from the character of home market demand and the forces which shaped it.

There was undoubtedly a contraction of aggregate demand on the home market which was the result of a number of factors. First, it reflected a fall in incomes and thus in purchasing power.[17] Secondly, it reflected an unwillingness on the part of some receivers of income to spend it. Under the first heading comes the decline in the total income of the large agrarian sector in real terms. Many peasants already made only a small contribution to the market by reason of their low cash incomes. The depression reduced their spending power still further, with repercussions for urban industry and the service trades.[18] The incomes of the artisan sector contracted in the same way, being in large part a function of demand from those concerned mainly with agriculture. The total sum of money paid out in wages shrank considerably. The labour force contracted by as much as two million; almost half a million were registered as unemployed in the depths of the depression and there was much short-time working.[19] Government deflationary measures also reduced the money incomes of some government employees and pensioners.

Source: *Ibid*. Table 47, p. 242.

It was estimated that in 1945 30 per cent of the stock of houses were over 100 years old; in 61 towns with over 30,000 inhabitants the average age of houses was 57 years and 19 per cent were over 100 years old.—Marc Aucy, 'Habitations et logement' *Revue d'économie politique,* lvii (1947), 1686.

17. The estimate of the total wage and salary bill (in billions of francs) made by L. Dugé de Bernonville, 'Revenus privés et consommations', *Rev. d'écon. pol.* lii (1939), gives the following results:

1930	1931	1932	1933	1934	1935	1936	1938
123·7	118·4	107·4	102·5	93·8	87·4	119·7	133·0

The cost of living was, of course, falling to 1936. The index of 213 articles constructed by J. Singer-Kérel, *Le Coût de la vie à Paris de 1840 à 1954;* Paris, 1961, fell 20·7 per cent in 1935 by comparison with 1930, and her statistics show all the indexes of real wages increasing until 1936; see p. 149.

18. According to calculations made by M. Auge-Laribé and published in an article in *Revue d'économie politique,* liii, 1939, p. 1174, the purchasing power of the agrarian sector fell after the war to 80 per cent of its 1913 level, which was not attained again until 1925. During the depression it fell to 86 per cent in 1931–32, to 77 per cent in 1934 and to 63 per cent in 1935 despite price supports, tariffs and quotas—or perhaps because of them.

19. *Unemployment in France (000's in receipt of benefit)*

1929	1930	1931	1932	1933	1934	1935	1936	1937	1938
0·9	2·4	54·6	273·8	276·3	341·6	425·8	433·7	351·3	374·1

Source: Sauvy, *op. cit.*, p. 554.

What happened to the incomes of property-owners, rentiers, professional people and the rest of the middle class is more difficult to say. Some sections, like the owners of rent-controlled property, probably lost. On the other hand, those on fixed incomes gained from falling prices. The effect on shareholders depended very much on what sort of shares they held, but overall industrial share prices tended to fall. However, there are signs that the recipients of property incomes, profits and dividends hoarded on a large scale or spent cautiously and then in the traditional ways.[20] Uncertainty about the future was a predominant factor in this situation.

Although aggregate demand was unfavourably affected by the depression that does not mean that individual incomes fell. Wherever the fall in prices exceeded the fall in money income there was obviously an increase in personal spending power. The signs of a small but steady improvement in living standards during the 'thirties indicates this.[21] Nevertheless, workers and civil servants resented reductions in money wages although compared with the pre-depression period they still might be better off in real terms. No one readily accepts a cut in income on such a basis; the reduction is still resented and those affected fight back, as the Flandin and Laval governments learned to their cost. For many people, such as civil servants, the depression period was thus one of a small rise in real incomes. This was true also of those workers who did not suffer from unemployment or short-time and were able to resist big cuts in money earnings. But there is also the question of what the higher

20. Many middle-class people held gold as a hedge against inflation, but large quantities of Bank of France notes were also held by the public. *The Economist*, 21 December 1935, quoted an article by P. Strohl, General Secretary of the Bank of France, which drew attention to the large-scale hoarding of newly issued notes of 500 and 1,000 francs denomination. It suggested that 'between 1928 and 1931 26,000 million of notes were issued against gold, which had been repatriated as a result of stabilisation and have since been hoarded through fear of various complications inherent in the economic and political crisis' p. 1257.
21. For instance, total meat consumption rose from 1,381,000 tons in 1928 to 1,535,000 tons in 1936, milk from 107·3 million hectolitres in 1929 to 128·9 million hectolitres in 1936, and groundnut oil from 186,000 tons in 1928 to 237,000 tons in 1936. On *per capita* consumption the calculations of L. Dugé de Bernonville yielded the following results: between 1928–30 and 1933–5 the increase for meat was 5·1 per cent, for potatoes 7·7 per cent, for coffee 7·5 per cent, for oranges and bananas 57 per cent, and for cooking oil 4·7 per cent. However, *per capita* consumption of beer, salt, and tobacco fell. See 'Les Salaires et les consommations', *Revue d'économie politique,* 1, (1936).

real incomes of the period consisted of. The evidence seems to suggest that they took the form mainly of more and better food and to some extent of services. They did not go to any great extent on manufactured goods or housing. One reason for this was perhaps that modern forms of merchandising and credit selling were poorly developed, especially by comparison with the Anglo-Saxon countries, so that the potential market for the new consumer durables remained largely untapped until after the war. This helps to explain the disappointing performance of the 'new' industries.

Involuntary unemployment, with the exception of brief periods such as the first year of the 1914–18 war, had never been a serious problem until the 'thirties.[22] Unlike Britain, the previous decade had seen not unemployment but labour scarcity, met both by continued movement from the land and by immigration. In the course of 1932 those in receipt of benefit exceeded a quarter of a million and at its peak the annual average reached 433,700 in 1936. The figures, high by French standards, seem modest by comparison with those recorded at this time in other advanced countries. Partly, no doubt, being traditionally less of a problem it was measured less accurately, the figures being collected on a departmental basis and the onus of relief falling on local authorities. Only those receiving assistance are included in the figures which therefore underestimate the numbers actually available for work. But the relatively modest total must also depend on other factors.

In the first place there was a serious contraction in the number of jobs, probably by something like two million. On the other hand the labour force also contracted. About 600,000 foreign workers left France. The ageing of the population plus accelerated retirement may have reduced the numbers seeking work by roughly the same number. The numbers of young recruits to the labour market were reduced both as a result of the low birth rate during and after the war and because juveniles stayed at school somewhat longer than before. A large part of the shrinkage in the number of jobs available can thus be accounted for

22. For a useful recent discussion of unemployment in the 1930s see J-C. Asselin, 'La semaine de 40 heures, le chômage et l'emploi', *Le Mouvement Social*, lii, 1966.

before the numbers receiving relief are brought into the picture. In addition, of course, some industries, such as textiles and clothing, practised systematic short-time working. For the rest, the existence of large peasant and artisan sectors meant that there was a great deal of hidden unemployment and underemployment which it would be difficult to calculate. Many urban workers went back to their families in the villages. Small producers and artisans who might otherwise have sought wage work hung on for exiguous returns and their ranks were joined by former wage-workers unable to find employment. In fact the unemployed accounted for in the figures of those receiving relief were heavily concentrated in the department of the Seine and a few industrial areas.[23] These knew, if on a smaller scale, the type of unemployment problems which was general in the industrial countries during the depression.

It should be added that a high proportion of the unemployed were older people (32 per cent were over fifty in 1936), women and unskilled men.[24] In other words, it could not be automatically absorbed by an expansion of industry or, to put it another way, the supply of industrial labour was more inelastic than appeared from the overall figures. This was a factor which the Popular Front government failed to take into account in 1936. Once recovery began industry soon experienced a shortage of skilled and semiskilled workers. This reflected the fact that enough of the former had not been trained and that many of the latter, being foreigners, had left France for their countries of origin.

The relatively modest scale of unemployment was thus a result of special conditions which reflected unfavourably on French capitalism rather than the reverse. Moreover, while unemployment in other countries was falling it continued to increase in France through to 1936 and remained well above the 1932 level until the war. This was symptomatic of a deep-seated stagnationist tendency, the obverse side of the virtual stagnation of manufacturing production and constructional activity. It was not merely a question of unemployment which could respond to specific

23. Asselin, *op. cit.*   24. *Ibid.*

measures but reflected the whole crisis of bourgeois society—
the demographic imbalance, the unwillingness of capitalists
to invest, of banks to lend money, of consumers to spend
more. The timidity of government policy, its adherence to
the *franc Poincaré* and its pursuit of budgetary equilibrium
were a product of the crisis and tended to prolong its
effects.

The situation would no doubt have been worse had the
policies of the Flandin and Laval governments, the most
energetic deflators, been more successful. In fact it proved
impossible to bring about a consistent deflation of costs and
incomes and for many real incomes continued to rise. The
deflations were, in any case, more budgetary than real,
more a question of book entries than of real government
economies. It was part of the depression that many tax
receipts tended to fall below government expectations
while certain forms of government expenditure tended to
rise. To meet the shortfall in revenue the government
resorted to backdoor methods of financing, namely by
short-term borrowing from the Bank of France.[25] As a
result the note circulation rose and purchasing power
increased. Deficit financing of this unintentional sort no
doubt contributed to the modest recovery of which there
were signs in the second half of 1935 and the first half of
1936. But the Laval government had already dug its grave
by its deflationary measures and was to be condemned by
the electorate despite this upturn in economic activity.

Although in retrospect devaluation appears as an elementary step to take before any of France's economic ills
could be tackled, it was opposed by virtually every interest
group at this time.[26] There was no question of its accept-
ance by the parliamentary majority elected in 1932.[27] No
party or coalition of parties which openly espoused it could
have hoped for success at the polls. Although the first Blum

25. As *The Economist* of 30 December 1935 put it: 'The fact is that the Government
and the Bank of France, despite their orthodox canon, have been driven by the
exigencies of the situation in the direction of credit expansion.' The persistence of
depression kept down budget receipts so that, despite economies in expenditure,
borrowing on short term from the Bank of France became inevitable. See also for a
discussion of this, Sauvy, *op. cit.*, ii, 165 f.
26. Perrot, *op. cit.*
27. *The Economist*, 11 Aug. 1934, noted that Reynaud's speech in the Chamber of
Deputies in favour of devaluation had received a cool reception and that not one paper
had taken up his views.

government had to devalue after about two months of office the prime minister had hoped to carry through a policy of 'reflation without devaluation'. When he decided to the contrary is not certain.[28] Some members of his party had concluded even before the election that it was inevitable, but it was not inscribed in the programme of the Popular Front. It was not acceptable to the small-property owners and rentiers who made up much of the clientele of the Radical Party. The Communist Party, anxious to preserve the coalition with the Radicals, strongly opposed devaluation before and after the election victory. Probably most workers and peasants were indifferent to the question. The last word no doubt lay with the big financial interests and their orthodox supporters in banking circles and in the administration.

Without devaluation the possibilities for recovery were strictly limited. French exports remained expensive, the cost of living appeared high to prospective visitors, and both French and foreign holders of funds were influenced by the fear that it might take place despite the government's intentions. A flight of capital began a year or so before the Popular Front took office. However, the Bank of France's gold reserves, although depleted by capital movements and gold outflow, were so large at this time that there was no question of the country being forced off the gold standard and into devaluation by a balance of payments crisis. The issue could have been decided *à froid,* as a matter of calculation, by a determined government. But it was not, and it could not have been, given the outlook of those in power. When Blum finally decided to take the plunge and throw off the incubus of the *franc Poincaré,* the step was taken *à chaud,* under pressure and with reluctance. It was too late and too little. The chance of sharing in the world trade recovery of the mid-thirties had been lost. French industry had fallen behind technologically through a failure to maintain the rate of investment. With costs increasing also under the influence of the new social

28. Some prominent members of the Socialist Party (SFIO) did support devaluation. Earlier, they had had to take into account the popularity of Poincaré's stabilisation. According to Baumgartner, later governor of the Bank of France, Léon Blum decided upon devaluation in the first fortnight of his government. See the colloquium *Léon Blum: Chef de Gouvernement* Paris, 1968, p. 281.

measures it found itself with only a small and temporary advantage from the first devaluation. World prices had been on the rise for some time.

Whatever criticisms may be levelled against the Popular Front, those which come from orthodox and conservative quarters often fail to recognise how deep was the responsibility of the preceding governments for prolonging and aggravating the depression. When Blum took over, avowedly to make capitalism work better than those who believed in it, he thus began with a heavy handicap. The French bourgeoisie and the governments it projected had been quite unable to understand the forces which had brought about the depression or elaborate ways of overcoming it. On the contrary, their responses tended to make it worse. The several efforts of the bourgeoisie, as private individuals and as firms, to safeguard their particular interests did more to accelerate the decline than to assist recovery. They cut back on investment, hoarded their spare funds and spent parsimoniously. At the least shock they sent their liquid funds in search of refuge abroad. They and their forebears had created a demographic pattern unfavourable to growth and which helped to sap the forces of enterprise and innovation without which their system would seize up. More than a cyclical decline, the 'thirties in France represented the crisis of a class and of a social structure which preserved its domination.

The performance of the French economy in the 'thirties was as disastrous as it had been brilliant in the previous decade. The automatic forces making for recovery which might have been expected operated only feebly. In part this was a result of the attempt to insulate France from the world market because, whatever it did to dampen the influence of the slump it also prevented the revival of world trade from having its full effects. The contraction of the labour force and the unfavourable demographic trends must be accorded some importance, but it is difficult to say how much. Self-sufficiency in basic foodstuffs became a handicap to recovery.[29] Measures to keep up farm prices, together with the fact that the working and middle classes did not get the benefits of a favourable shift in the terms of trade

29. About 80 per cent of the French calorific intake came from home sources.

towards manufactured goods which would have followed and reduced the cost of living had they been able to buy food at world prices, limited the possible growth of the internal market and checked the growth of French exports. There was little tendency for demand to be shifted to the products of 'new' industries and thus encourage a higher rate of investment which would have contributed to recovery despite a tendency for real income per head to rise.

In some respects it may be true that the preservation, by interference with market forces, of a large agrarian sector still largely in the hands of small cultivators, enabled the country to avoid some of the more dramatic consequences of the depression. Unemployment was not so heavy, poverty and distress less widespread than in countries which were more thoroughly industrialised. Agriculture, for all that it suffered from low prices and low incomes, acted as something of a cushion. Traditionalists continued to extol the virtues of rural life in an anachronistic manner; even economists spoke of 'the balance' of the French economy. Looking more deeply, the preservation of this agrarian sector was heavily bought and the failure to recover from the depression showed it. It helped to keep down incomes, restrict the growth of the home market, discourage investment and limit the possibilities of export revival. It gave to French capitalism a lack of flexibility and response to change which might not be too serious in a period of expansion but became dominant in a period of contraction. It thus reinforced the inflexibility which all the older industrial countries demonstrated as a result of over-investment in the older forms of technology with a specially powerful inbuilt check which inhibited even the 'normal' cyclical tendencies towards recovery which appear after a period of depression. It was part of the setup that most policy measures tended to perpetuate the old structures, to protect the *situations acquises,* rather than to break them up and promote a new expansion. It took another disastrous war and the upset which it produced to clear the way for that.

9

THE BLUM EXPERIMENT
1936–37

I

The economic and social policies of the first year of the
Popular Front government elected in May 1936 marked a
distinctive period in French economic history.[1] Largely
failing in their immediate purpose, they nevertheless left a
permanent mark; they broke with the deflationary policies
of the previous five years and established the foundations of
a welfare state. At the time they appeared to be the French
counterpart of the New Deal: an attempt to use new
methods to break out of the depression. If the New Deal
was identified with Roosevelt, the Popular Front was
identified with Léon Blum, and this year of policy-making
can with aptness be described as 'the Blum experiment'.[2]

The victory of the Popular Front came as a reaction to

1. There is no really good account of the Popular Front in English; the contemporary
reportage by A. Werth, *The Destiny of France* (London, 1937) conserves an interest.
See also, A. Mitzman, 'The French working class and the Blum Government', *The
International Review of Social History*, ix, no. 3, 1964. The most comprehensive
recent French work is G. Lefranc, *Histoire du Front Populaire* (Paris, 1964). See also,
D. Guérin, *Front Populaire, révolution manquée* (Paris, 1963). These works are
mainly concerned with the politics of the Popular Front.
2. See the report of the colloquium, *Léon Blum: Chef de Gouvernement*, especially
the contributions of J-M. Jeanneney and P. Mendès-France. Also, the comment by
J. Bouvier, 'Un débat toujours ouvert: la politique économique du Front populaire' in
Le Mouvement Social, no. 54, Jan-Mars, 1966.

years of deflation and depression as well as anxiety at the rising tide of fascism in Europe which found expression in the activities of the fascist leagues in France itself. Even before Blum took office a large-scale and spontaneous strike movement accompanied by the occupation of factories and other places of work in May 1936 showed that the working class was intent on great changes. Blum later described this as a slap in the face; it was more like a pistol pointed at the government to insist that it take action against the capitalists, many of whom were deeply shaken, even demoralised, by the turn of events. The crisis of confidence in the ruling class and the deep desire for change, even though it might not assume a consciously revolutionary form, which swept the working class in the wake of the Popular Front electoral victory made the situation potentially revolutionary. The defusing of this explosive potential was a delicate task carried on at the level of government and in negotiations it initiated between the *patronat* and the trade unions, and in the factories and among the workers, where the task was confided to the CGT and especially the Communist Party.[3] The first led to the Matignon Agreement and a series of statutes concerning hours of work, holidays with pay, collective bargaining and other social and economic reforms passed in June and August 1936. It is with these and their effects that the present discussion will be principally concerned.

II

Something must be said, to begin with, about Léon Blum's approach to the situation in which he found himself.[4] At the head of a coalition which had won its victory thanks to the support not only of the Communist Party but also of the Radicals, he had no intention either before or during his term of office of stepping outside the confines of capitalist

3. The fusion of the Communist-led *Confédération Générale du Travail Unitaire* with the *Confédération Générale du Travail* from which it had split away in 1922 in March 1936, had strengthened the position of the Communist Party in the unions, especially in the big factories.
4. For the formation of Blum's thought see H. Ziebura, *Léon Blum et le parti socialiste, 1872–1934*, Paris, 1968.

property relations. In this he drew with him the major part of his own party, the Socialist Party (SFIO), in which he enjoyed considerable authority, and received the support of the Communist Party, which considered it imperative to conciliate the Radical wing of the Popular Front. The Radicals were heterogeneous in their views, but they were based socially on the middle class and were supporters of capitalism and of parliamentary institutions whatever reforms they might have thought desirable in view of the crisis they were then passing through. Blum had conceived of such a situation long before, when the SFIO began to enter into electoral pacts with other parties. He therefore drew a distinction between the 'exercise of power', in which the party would have no mandate to introduce socialist measures, and the 'conquest of power' in which, with a solid majority, it would proceed to implement its programme. The Popular Front was clearly of the former type: he was thus called upon to act as a loyal manager[5] of the affairs of capitalism, however little the way he performed this function was appreciated by the capitalist supporters of the right wing parties now unaccustomedly in opposition and confronted with what they rightly thought to be the threat of revolution.

In saying that Blum had never given much attention to a detailed study of economic problems, as distinct from those budgetary and monetary problems which had occupied the forefront of French politics since the end of the war, is only to emphasise how typical he was of most French politicians of his day, even those of the left.[6] He had, however, picked up from the interminable discussions about the causes of the economic depression some basic ideas and a panacea. The root cause of the crisis was a lack of purchasing power in the hands of the masses: by placing more money in their hands the grip of economic stagnation could be overcome. It was assumed that the goodwill of the capitalists could be obtained for measures of this kind, without making any inroads into capitalist property. The somewhat sketchy

---

5. The phrase he used at the Riom trial was 'un gérant loyal'.
6. According to Sauvy, Blum was 'peu familier avec les questions économiques, ignorant à peu près tout des statistiques et des indices (et tout le parti avec lui) ...' *Hist. écon.*, ii, p. 230. He was apparently not aware of the upturn in industrial production which had begun in the autumn of 1935.

programme of the Popular Front was based on these assumptions.[7] It neither put forward detailed proposals for a planned economy nor offered the prospect of nationalising the basic industries and big industrial firms. To do so would have made an alliance with the Radicals impossible. This 'moderation' was not merely endorsed by the Communist Party: it was insistent that the programme should not go beyond the bounds of mild reforms.

Faced on assuming office with the danger of revolution and civil war Blum pushed ahead with this programme as fast as possible and was, indeed, obliged to go further in concessions to the working class than had been originally intended or envisaged in the programme of the Popular Front. The first step taken was the meeting between government representatives, trade union leaders and officials of the employers' organisation which issued in the Matignon Agreement. Blum promised that legislation would soon be passed concerning holidays-with-pay, the forty-hour week and collective bargaining. With that accepted, the employers agreed to increase wages from the time that the strikes were brought to an end from between 7 and 15 per cent (not more than a 12 per cent increase in the total wage bill for any one enterprise).[8] Agreements later made with the unions carried this understanding into effect. Within a few days, after strenuous efforts by the trade union leaders and all the support the Communist Party could muster, workers began to leave the mines and factories.[9] Nevertheless, a month after the Matignon Agreement over 100,000 workers were still in occupation of the factories.

The industrialists had to pay a heavy price, in their eyes, to get their property returned to them and their authority recognised again. Given the determination and the spirit of

7. For the programme of its forebear, the *Rassemblement Populaire*, see Lefranc, *Histoire du Front Populaire*, pp. 441–5.
8. G. Lefranc, *Le Mouvement syndical sous la Troisième République*, Paris, 1967, ch. 7, *passim*.
9. This was the occasion for the speech by Maurice Thorez telling the workers that they 'must know how to end a strike' and that 'compromise' was necessary 'if all the demands have not yet been accepted but if victory has been obtained on the most essential and important demands'. The Communist leaders worked hard to bring the strikes to a speedy end both in Paris and in the provinces. See D. R. Brower, *The New Jacobins*, New York, 1968, pp. 152–3. For left critics of the party line see P. Broué and N. Dorey, 'Critiques de gauche et opposition révolutionnaire au front populaire (1936–37)', in *Le Mouvement Social*, no. 54, jan-mars, 1966.

the workers the factories could not have been evacuated by force, despite the evident illegality of the sit-in strikes. It was only by concessions in wages and promises of legislative reform, combined with the persuasive powers of the leaders of the trade unions and the Communist Party, that the strike could be brought to an end, and with it the prospect of revolution.[10]

Blum inherited, as has already been shown, an overvalued franc for which, in purely economic terms, the obvious remedy was devaluation. Devaluation did not appear in the Popular Front programme and there was a good deal of difference of opinion about its advisability in government circles. Blum hoped to be able to reflate without devaluation, but some of the economists sympathetic to his government thought otherwise. Being wise after the event it is easy to say that Blum should have announced from the start that he intended to devalue and should have proceeded to do so as soon as possible after taking office.[11] In fact it was delayed until September, and by that time further out-flows of gold and currency had taken place. The adoption of a more realistic exchange rate increased the possibility for recovery by cheapening French exports and encouraging tourism. Once a new exchange rate had been established there was also a possibility that some of the funds which had taken refuge in foreign markets would find their way back to Paris.

The wage increases of June and the legislation of August, when its effects began to appear, were bound to increase industrial costs. But they had a variety of untoward effects which contradicted the sanguine expectations Blum had placed in the increase in purchasing power as a stimulant to recovery. In the first months the increase in costs came

10. Was there a 'revolutionary situation' in France in May-June, 1936? The question was to have its echo thirty-two years later. See the views expressed during the colloquium, *Léon Blum . . .*, cited above.
11. Again there are differences of opinion about when Blum decided that devaluation was inevitable. Georges Monnet was sent to Washington to clear the ground and London was probably informed in the middle of August.

from higher wages and paid holidays, as the forty-hour week did not generally become effective until industrial agreements were worked out. Employers were generally unprepared to assimilate such measures because of the neglect of investment in the previous years. Where they could do so the higher costs were passed on directly to their customers. Smaller and weaker enterprises may have responded by cutting their labour force. While increased money wages stimulated some industries, such as textiles and food, it was as an increase in costs that they were bound to be mainly felt by industry as a whole. In addition, the higher money incomes encouraged a growth of imports and thus worsened an already adverse merchandise trade balance. By December retail prices were 17 per cent higher than in May.[12]

A sustained industrial recovery could only be based on a rise in profit expectations. The real source of French industrial weakness lay in the low profitability of investment and the dampening effects of an overvalued currency, deflation and years of government parsimony. As already pointed out, the recovery which had begun in 1935 and the first half of 1936 was connected with the fact that the government had, despite its declared deflationary intentions, been adding to liquidity by increasing the volume of Treasury Bills discounted by the Bank of France.[13] Again, being wise after the event, it can be claimed that Blum would have been more successful had he gone straight for deficit financing—together with a sufficiently large devaluation—and measures to raise industrial investment and reduce costs. The obstacles to this were his Radical allies and his need to conciliate orthodox opinion on the one side and the irresistible claims of the working class on the other. The choices open to Blum were thus much more restricted than some of his critics at the time and since seem to

12. This represented an annual rate of 25 per cent, or from September to December of 60 per cent: 'les records des pires moments des années 20 sont battus et ce rythme est même largement supérieur à celui des années de guerre', Sauvy, *Hist. écon.* ii, 234.
13. As *The Economist* of 29 Feb. 1936 put it: 'The deflation of the French economy came to an end last autumn, not by design but by force of circumstances. The volume of defence expenditure thought necessary, together with the railway and other deficits, created a situation in which something like £200 million a year was being spent by the Government over and above the sums raised in taxation. The stimulating effect of this expenditure was such that, despite a high rate of interest, business began to recover.'

suggest. His greatest illusion was no doubt his confidence that capitalists would cooperate in carrying out a policy which was so obviously reasonable and moderate.[14] In fact he was deeply mistrusted however loyally he carried out the exercise of power.[15]

While it is clear that employers were discouraged from expanding production and embarking on new investment by the higher costs resulting from wage increases and the forty-hour week, this was a contradiction inherent in Blum's policy. French capitalism in its existing state, confronting a strong working class, would not have been able to reduce costs and restore the former forty-eight-hour week except by authoritarian means. The 'exercise of power' meant attempting to devise some policy which would satisfy the demands of the working class, win the cooperation of the capitalists and enable the Popular Front government to conserve a majority in the Assembly while at the same time persuading a hostile Senate to pass its legislation. These aims were impossible to reconcile. The failure of devaluation to give the economy a permanent boost was a big blow to Blum's hopes.[16] The continued outflow of capital meanwhile demonstrated that he had been unable to reassure the property-owners. So far as a worsening foreign exchange position accumulated further difficulties for the government it is possible to argue that failure to impose exchange control was a fatal weakness of policy.[17] The main reason why it was not applied was that it was supposed that it would have been virtually impossible to enforce without authoritarian methods. In fact the door was left open for capital movements as a concession to the bourgeoisie—and

14. G. Dupeux, 'L'échec du premier gouvernement Léon Blum', *Revue d'histoire moderne et contemporaine*, x, jan.–mars, 1963.
15. Distrusted both as a socialist and as a Jew: anti-semitism was rampant in right-wing circles and in the previous year Blum had been physically attacked by a crowd of royalists.
16. In fact the devaluation did stimulate the economy at first but rising costs and prices rapidly counteracted its effects.
17. As one critic puts it '*Either* the Blum Government should have insisted on its radical policy, even if it meant forcing the capitalists into submission by exchange control or more vigorous measures if necessary *or* it should have provided the conditions in which the mainspring of the capitalist economy, the profit motive of the entrepreneurs, would effectively function'.—H. W. Arndt, *The Economic Lessons of the Nineteen Thirties*, 2nd ed, London, 1963, p. 149 and see the whole of ch. 5. But the first alternative meant social revolution—no longer the 'exercise of power'; the second the defeat of the working class which in 1936 and early 1937 would have fought back. See Mitzman, *op. cit.*, and Broué and Dorey, *op. cit.*

this failed in its purpose. It was not purely a technical question but one of social forces. The Popular Front government was a prisoner of its own limitations: that it could only operate a reform programme designed to make capitalism work, and only then so far as the bourgeoisie was prepared to accept it, or feared that if it did not worse would follow.

During the first months of Blum's government the effects of the strikes and the wage increases and paid holidays conceded in the Matignon Agreement were to raise prices while production fell. Industrial costs were increased by higher wages without the expected stimulus to the economy which would have enabled them to be spread over an increased output as some optimists hoped. The increased demand for consumer goods and services also tended to raise their prices while imports increased. Meanwhile the flight from the franc continued. Despite the outflow of gold, however, the reserves remained above the danger level. The case for devaluation rested on a different basis, namely the overvaluation of the franc and its depressive effects on the economy. Blum seems to have hesitated to devalue, partly because of the bad reception it was likely to have on middle-class public opinion in France, partly because he did not wish to take a step which might be opposed by the United States and Britain. It was only after the matter had been discussed with the governments of these countries that the final decision was made.

Already, by a law of 24 July 1936 the Bank of France was brought under state control. Hitherto governed by its two hundred largest shareholders—probable origin of the popular phrase 'the two hundred families'—its Assembly was now open to all shareholders and the place of the Regents was taken by a council appointed by the government.[18] This change was intended to increase the influence of the state over the credit system. It was not a measure of nationalisation properly speaking; the rest of the banking system remained in private hands and the so-called *mur d'argent* was unbreached.

Devaluation came with the law of 1 October, after agreement had been reached with London and Washington. It

18. Sauvy, *Hist. écon.*, ii, p. 213, Lefranc, *Hist. du Front Populaire*, pp. 369–71.

was presented as an 'alignment' of the franc with the dollar and the pound sterling devalued respectively three and five years before. The franc was devalued by a little over 25 per cent compared with the *franc Poincaré* which was too little to achieve this object as well as being too late. According to the law owners of more than 200 grammes of gold were to hand it in to the Bank of France at the pre-devaluation rate and all gold transactions were subject to its approval.[19] An Exchange Stabilisation Fund was established, able to intervene in the exchange market to stabilise the franc within its new legal limits. At the same time the free movement of capital, other than gold, was guaranteed: in other words the government forswore the weapon of exchange control in deference to holders of liquid funds.

The new measures gave only a temporary check to the outflow of capital seeking refuge abroad which was resumed during the autumn and winter. By the end of January 1937 the gold deposited with the Exchange Stabilisation Fund had been exhausted in trying to counter this movement. Vincent Auriol, Blum's Finance Minister, considered that the time was ripe for a further devaluation. In fact the results of the devaluation of October 1936 did not come up to expectations. The step was badly received in most quarters and the reason for it was misunderstood. The main benefits could be expected to accrue to the export industries: for the first time for five years French prices had become competitive. At the same time, the growing imports now cost more. But it was the continued pressure on prices arising from the wage increases of June 1936, coupled now with the effects of the forty-hour week as it became applicable in one industry after another in the last month or two of 1936 and early in 1937, which was decisive. Within a short time, therefore, the stimulating effect of devaluation had worn itself out. The flight of capital continued.

IV

During the early months of 1937 it became evident that neither the policy of raising purchasing power nor devalua-

19. Neurisse, A., *Histoire du franc*, Paris, 1967, pp. 76–8.

tion on the scale carried out by Auriol in September 1936, was able to overcome the economic stagnation. At the root of the trouble was the continued lack of confidence in business circles and the adverse effect on profits of the higher wages and shorter hours won by the strikes of June 1936. As the forty-hour agreements came into force wage bills rose by something like 20 per cent and these higher costs were again passed on in higher prices. The limitation of hours had no appreciable effect on unemployment. The unemployed included few skilled men able to fill vacancies in the factories created by the limitation of hours.[20] Production was therefore held back or curtailed by labour scarcity and costs rose. Employers complained of lower productivity and loss of authority in industry in the period following the strike. The labour disputes which held up the Exposition of 1937 was an example. Workers were now resisting the authoritarian methods which, before June 1936, prevailed over much of French industry.[21]

Supporters of capitalism have argued that the first priority for recovery was the prospect of higher profits. Higher wages would then have been possible. According to them, Blum required an impossible act of faith on the part of employers in seeing higher wages and the growth of demand thereby created as the motive force of recovery. While it is true that Blum did hope that raising purchasing power would enable the depression to be overcome, it is obvious that his hand was forced by the irruption of the working class on to the scene in May and June 1936. The higher costs and industrial difficulties of 1937, however unwelcome to industrialists and however much they prevented recovery, were in fact the alternative to revolution. What was at issue was at no time merely differing techniques for making capitalism work.[22]

In practice the Blum experiment neither satisfied the working class nor won the confidence of the bourgeoisie.

20. Asselin, 'La semaine de 40 heures . . .', *loc. cit.*
21. Membership of trade unions grew sensationally from about a million and a quarter early in 1936 to nearly five million by the end of the year; the occupation of factories, practised in May 1936, gave the workers a new sense of power.
22. For technical discussions of the economic aspects of Blum's policy see, for example, the contemporary articles by M. Kalecki, 'Lessons of the Blum experiment' *Economic Journal* xlvii, March 1938 and the hostile critique by M. Marjolin, 'Reflections on the Blum experiment' in *Economica* v, no. 18, May 1938.

Not only did it fail to make inroads into capitalist property or install a planned economy, but the material gains won by the working class were soon largely lost, swallowed up by rising prices. Those which remained—paid holidays and the legal forty-hour week in particular—were not only the most obnoxious to the employers but the ones which have been most strongly criticised on technical grounds, i.e. that they held back industrial production and therefore the rise in real incomes.[23] On the other hand, what French capitalism most required was the restoration of confidence in the franc and still more in the future social stability of the country and in European peace. Conditions were lacking for such confidence. France's position in Europe had suffered a sharp decline with the rise of Nazi Germany: her governments lost their initiative in the international field and could only choose between the Anglo-Saxons and the fascist bloc. Confidence in the prospects of investment at home—though it showed signs of recovery in 1938–39 on the basis of government armament orders—was not in Blum's power to create in 1936–37. It was impossible to create the conditions for increased profitability without taking back the gains made by the working class, weakening the unions and re-establishing the authority of the *patronat*.

The Blum experiment died a lingering death in the spring of 1937. By this time the forty-hour week had become effective and the index of industrial production, after reaching a peak in March, began to fall. In February Leon Blum announced the 'pause' in the social programme of the Popular Front. The change of course represented, perhaps more than anything else, Blum's lack of confidence in his own solutions for the crisis after some seven months 'exercise of power'. The economic programme of the government, including public works, education and aid to agriculture, greatly increased expenditure which was also rising under the pressure of armaments. The prospect of a large budget deficit therefore came into view.[24] The

23. This is the burden of Sauvy's critique in *op. cit.* ch., 17. The reduction of hours came at the wrong time and it was too great. Despite Sauvy's 'progressive' alternative outlined in his book, his critique does not differ very much from those of all sections of conservative opinion at the time.
24. Foreign policy acted as a further constraint on economic and social reform at home. As Lefranc expresses it, 'Léon Blum ne peut entreprendre aucune politique

pressures of financial orthodoxy began to assert themselves. In March a large National Defence loan issue was launched enabling the lender to choose the dollar or the pound, as well as the franc, as the money of account by which the capital of the loan was to be reimbursed and interest paid. This was an attempt to encourage the return of capital to France, a big concession to holders of funds, and a recognition of the government's dependence upon the old financial methods. In the same month the right of free dealing in gold including its exportation, was re-established.[25] The capitulation to the *mur d'argent* was complete.

The Blum experiment was thus no bold venture into deficit financing. It was quickly returned to the limits of financial orthodoxy. It failed to take the most elementary measures against capital movements. The restrictions on gold movements were ended after only a few months and gold exports were resumed on a considerable scale. By June the Bank of France was losing gold rapidly and the Exchange Equilisation Fund had again exhausted its reserves. The franc came under heavy pressure and the bank rate was raised. Blum, and his Finance Minister, Vincent Auriol, worked out a project to check the prospective budget deficit without a big increase in taxation. The resignation of three leading economists from the Council of the Bank of France as a result of their disagreement with government policy enhanced a growing tension in the Chambers and in the country at large. Blum asked for and received from the Chamber of Deputies a mandate to invoke special powers to deal with the financial crisis. After a lengthy and acrimonious debate in the Senate the government's request was defeated by a large majority, whereupon Léon Blum resigned.

The debate on 'the Blum experiment' and on the Popular Front continues. Any balance-sheet of its attempt to solve the problems of the depression which it inherited from its

financière qui le coup de Londres et de Washington. Il n'est pas lié seulement par le contrat qu'est pour lui le programme du Front Populaire. Il est paralysé par la situation internationale'.—*Histoire du Front Populaire*, pp. 230–1.

25. Law of 8 March 1937, which permitted holders of gold to retain the increase in value which at the time of devaluation was supposed to be paid to the Treasury; those who had surrendered their gold were paid the difference. See, e.g. Neurrisse, *op. cit.*, p. 77.

predecessors must be provisional. Professional economists have been generally critical of Blum's economic policy. Even a writer like Lefranc, sympathetic on the whole to Blum, concludes that economically the Popular Front failed: not only did it not bring about recovery but it actually compromised it.[26] Sauvy concentrates his fire on the reduction of working hours and Blum's economic illusions: he must be considered '*un grand homme mal informé*'.[27] Other economists have cast their criticisms more in the form of a requisitory: Blum's economic measures therefore read like a catalogue of errors.[28] What is often missing is the politics, more, the class bias, involved in the question. The economics of the Popular Front cannot be separated from its politics. But Blum set out to make capitalism work: that is what his concept of the 'exercise of power' meant. He only realised later, perhaps, that even when a left-wing government is in office in France the bourgeoisie continues to hold power. Shaken and even to some extent demoralised in May–June 1936, the bourgeoisie then sought to revenge itself not only on the trade unions and the working class but also on the government which it identified with the concessions which that class had won.[29]

The 'Blum experiment' failed, it may be said, not primarily because it employed wrong techniques to reflate an ailing capitalism rendered almost decrepit by half a decade of stagnation.[30] Its failure was political and in the circumstances it could only be an interim government before either a decided shift to the left or a relapse into reaction. Politics determined that the second alternative should be the one France was to follow. To analyse the reasons for this would go far beyond the limits of this work and impose an examination of the relationship of forces in

26. Lefranc, *Hist. du Front Populaire*, p. 340: 'Economiquement, on doit conclure à un échec du Front Populaire. Il n'a pas réussi le redressement qu'il espérait réaliser; il l'a sans doute compromis.'
27. Sauvy, *Hist. econ.*, ii, p. 307.
28. See J.-M. Jeanneney's contribution to the colloquium cited in note 2.
29. The main employers' organisation, which had negotiated the Matignon agreement with the unions, soon changed its name, and its spokesmen, and adopted a harder line. Funds began to flow into the coffers of De la Rocque's *Parti Social Français* and the more openly fascist *Parti Populaire Français* led by Jacques Doriot, a former leader of the Communist Party.
30. There is the view, of course, that if only Keynesian techniques for dealing with depression had been known . . . But it is doubtful whether they could have been used in the France of the 1930s.

French society, the position of the parties which made up the Popular Front and, in particular, the role played by the Communist Party in restraining the working class in and after the strikes of 1936. But the final epitaph on the Popular Front government must be that it expressed in the most acute form the dilemma of the whole of European social democracy in the epoch before the Second World War. It awakened hopes that could not be fulfilled within the framework of capitalism just as, at a decisive moment, it put up barriers to the revolutionary wave of 1936. It earned not gratitude but contempt from the bourgeoisie for its services and Blum became the most execrated man in the salons of France. Only in the working class did the 'conquests' and the *coude-à-coude* remain to be celebrated and remembered when the harsh reality of the defeat had been forgotten.

10

THE PROBLEMS OF
AGRICULTURE

It was characteristic of French capitalism in the twentieth century that it conserved a substantial agrarian sector in which the peasantry continued to play a dominant role. The industrialisation of the economy, with its improvement in communications and growth of urban population, had steadily extended the market for agricultural produce. Surely but unevenly, therefore, the mass of the peasantry, and not simply the larger, specialised producers and wine-growers, were drawn more completely into a market economy. Yet, down to the First World War and beyond, the basic structure of rural economy remained much as it had emerged from the Revolution, conserving in its organisation, as well as in the mentality of the cultivators, many anachronistic, precapitalist traits remarkable in an advanced capitalist country. The penetration of market relations into the peasant sector was a long drawn out and painful process. By necessity or by choice much production was carried on for use within the household. The great mass of the peasantry toiled excessively and lived badly. At the same time, the inability of the ruling class to promote a reorganisation of the agrarian economy limited the growth of the economy as a whole and strengthened other archaic traits, such as the survival of much small-scale artisan production. In particular, the low purchasing power of the mass of the peasants limited the extent of the home market for manufactured goods.

On the eve of the war agriculture continued to occupy about 43 per cent of the active male population. In 1911, of a population of 39·1 million, 22·1 million were classified as 'rural', though this does not mean employed in or directly dependent on agriculture. The weight of agriculture in the economy, despite the steady decline observable in the previous thirty-five years, was still considerable. It was characteristic that the property-owning peasants and small cultivators—leaseholders and *métayers*—were responsible for husbandry over a large part of the country. In fact, however, large landed proprietors continued to dominate the scene in about a quarter of the country and in many regions the local 'notables' came from landowning families descended from the traditional nobility or from bourgeois who had acquired land by purchase, notably by the acquisition of *biens nationaux* during the Revolution. French rural society was far from being egalitarian.[1] Economic differences within the peasantry were considerable. Many small property-owners owned only enough land to eke out a bare subsistence living at the price of interminable toil, or had to work for wages. A large part of the land, and of the marketable surplus, was in the hands of a smaller number of more prosperous peasants. Moreover, as specialised production developed in the latter part of the nineteenth century, whether on peasant land or on farms leased by the big estate owners, access to capital and credit became a crucial factor and a hired labour force was necessary; capitalist agriculture was steadily making headway.

It was clearly where production for the market was most advanced that French agriculture displayed its most modern traits. In the newer wine-producing areas of Languedoc, on the large wheat farms and where sugar-beet and industrial crops were produced, as in the north and the Paris Basin,

---

1. 'L'image classique d'un monde rural égalitaire comporte une fort part de mythologie ...', P. Barral, 'Aspects régionaux de l'agrarisme français avant 1930', *Le Mouvement Social*, no. 67, avril–juin, 1969.

production was on a larger scale and commercial middlemen played a key role. It was in such areas that up-to-date methods of cultivation were employed: farm machinery, fertilisers, modern buildings. Crop yields compared not too unfavourably with those in Britain or western Europe. This modernised sector stood out against the prevailing routinism and inefficiency which characterised much of peasant agriculture. It also meant that in some areas there was a sizeable agricultural proletariat, trade unions and labour disputes. Moreover, to make good a labour scarcity which was apparent even before the First World War, the larger farms and vineyards employed immigrant labour.

II

Lack of specialisation was a besetting weakness of peasant agriculture. Much land was devoted to the cultivation of wheat and other cereals which would have been better used for other purposes or left in permanent grass. This was indicated by the abysmally low yields in the least fertile areas and the low national figures for yield per acre compared with neighbouring countries.[2] On the other hand, where there were large farms and bigger and more prosperous peasant holdings yields reached a more respectable level.[3] There was some shift away from cereal production to livestock rearing in the wake of the fall in cereal prices which had characterised the agricultural depression of the last quarter of the nineteenth century. But this experience had produced as its main response high tariffs on imported food, and it could be argued that this policy contributed to the inefficiency of French agriculture, though it mainly assisted the big producers by keeping up their profits. At the other end of the scale, protection did nothing for the many peasant households who, through lack of means or knowledge, continued to produce the major part of their food requirements.

2. See the figures for yields cited in ch. 9, n. 21.
3. Yields in the north compared with those in the good farming areas of western Europe; areas like the Massif Central and the south-east, with their extremely low yields, brought down the national average. It was in such areas that much land was kept in cereal production which ought, on technical grounds, to have been turned over to permanent grass or other crops or abandoned altogether.

The basic economic defect of French agriculture, which held back its modernisation and retarded the growth of the economy as a whole, was the very characteristic which appeared to many to be its major virtue—the wide distribution of landed property. The majority of the peasant holdings were too small to function as efficient productive units and were further handicapped by consisting often of tiny and scattered strips and plots acquired by inheritance, marriage or purchase.[4] However, the development of market relations and their penetration into the villages promoted involved and contradictory reactions among the peasantry. On the one hand many, and not always the propertyless and the young, left the uncertainties and hardships of rural life for the promise of the towns with the new and varied job opportunities they offered, the higher and more secure incomes, and the improved amenities. On the other hand, others grasped all the more eagerly at the supposed security and shelter from the rigours of the market economy which the ownership of property seemed to offer or sought to take advantage of the new opportunities it held out by turning to more specialised production.

The 'rural exodus' of the late nineteenth century had caused much concern to politicians and publicists because the peasantry had always been seen as a conservative barrier to urban revolution. However, the measures taken to assist the peasantry remained puny. Protection benefited mainly the industrialists and large estate owners who prompted it. The great majority of the peasants, particularly those who most needed such facilities, remained outside the scope of agricultural cooperative and credit schemes down to 1914. There was nothing deserving of the description of an agricultural policy in this period.[5] The methods of economic liberalism prevailed even when they proved destructive of the social order which it was intended to defend. But

4. 'La division "democratique" de la propriété agricole a été poussée jusqu'à l'excès. Non seulement les surfaces dont les cultivateurs disposent sont petites, mais elles sont émiettées en beaucoup de petites parcelles. C'est là une caractéristique ancienne de la structure économique agricole française; il ne semble pas malheureusement qu'elle ait beaucoup changé', M. Augé-Laribé, 'Structure agricole' *Revue d'économie politique*, liii, no. 1. jan.–mars, 1939, p. 125.
5. M. Augé-Laribé, *La Politique agricole de la France de 1880 à 1940*, Paris, 1950, pp. 291–300. He concludes; 'La politique agricole de 1880 à 1914 a mal su, mollement voulu, pauvrement exécuté ce qui eût été nécessaire'.

economic forces were too weak to drive on the proletarianisation of the peasantry at a fast enough rate to permit the dominance of large-scale capitalist farming over the bulk of the agrarian sector. The small-scale unit thus remained predominant, despite the importance which the larger farms played as contributors to the marketable surplus.

In fact, French agriculture in the first decade or so of the twentieth century presents a more varied picture than is often supposed. There was a definite capitalist sector made up of large producers leasing land from the big estate owners and including the more prosperous peasants in which productivity levels were high. In the more backward areas, however, cultivation and methods of living remained archaic. In some areas a growing labour force of wage-workers had emerged and there was much temporary labour employed at peak periods. But there was, undoubtedly, over a large part of the country a predominance of small and medium-sized peasant holdings employing mainly family labour. Many of those who worked for wages did so in the expectation that they would eventually inherit a plot, acquire one by marriage or purchase or at least be able to rent one on a cash or *métayage* basis.

Before 1914 French agriculture provided the bulk of the nation's supply of basic foodstuffs. It did so, however, with the help of tariff protection which insulated high-cost producers from the effects of foreign competition. It meant that labour and resources were held in a markedly backward agrarian order which could have yielded more in terms of output had they been transferred elsewhere. French capitalism paid a price for its historical dependence on the peasantry in its struggle against feudalism and the belief of all sections of the property-owning classes that it was a socially conservative force which had to be preserved.

The immediate prewar years had been a period of mild prosperity for agriculture as it sloughed off the effects of the depression and benefited from the upsurge of industry. No doubt this prosperity was unequally distributed and felt most of all by those who were geared to production for the market. Structurally all the inherited weaknesses remained, resistant to market forces and largely undiscerned by policy-makers and public opinion. When the war began agriculture was as little prepared as any other part of the economy to meet its requirements. It was expected that if war should come existing stocks and requisitioning from current production would be sufficient to supply the needs of the army. Nothing was planned to deal with the production and distribution problems of a long war.

In fact, no sector of the economy was more profoundly affected by the new conditions of warfare than was agriculture.[6] Blanket mobilisation rapidly stripped it of its active manpower in 1914 leaving the rest of that summer's harvest to be gathered in by the womenfolk and those too old or too young to be called to the colours. The scarcity of labour was to be its besetting wartime problem. The military machine imposed other demands, as it was to do throughout the war, in its characteristically heavy-handed and, for the peasant, bewildering fashion; taking horses and other draught animals, requisitioning cattle and crops. Meanwhile the transport system was clogged with military traffic, making it difficult for agriculturalists to maintain contact with their markets and their suppliers. Before long shortages of every kind began to make themselves felt, above all the lack of fertilisers. And from the national point of view, the most disastrous blow of all was the invasion of the north and east, where the most productive food-producing areas were situated.

As the war dragged on the scarcity of labour led to a further reduction in the area under crops.[7] The government faced the problem at first by exhorting the peasant women and others left on the land to work harder. It later took other measures, releasing some conscripted peasants for work on the land, drafting in other soldiers and recruiting immigrant labour and prisoners of war for farm work. However, total output continued to decline. Crop yields were adversely affected by lack of fertilisers, the requisi-

6. M. Augé-Laribé, and P. Pinot, *Agriculture and Food Supply in France During the War* New Haven, 1927, a translation of two independent monographs of which the French originals appeared separately under the auspices of the Carnegie Trust.
7. Augé-Laribé and Pinot, *op. cit.*, ch. 2, *passim*.

tioning of draught animals and less skilled and intensive cultivation. Labour, especially that of women and girls, continued to be attracted from the land by the higher earnings available in war industry. In fact the government was never able to work out and apply a coherent war agricultural programme. With the help of imports it sought to keep prices down. The main crops were requisitioned for government purchase at fixed prices. By these means peasants and farmers were prevented from realising the profits from the higher prices which would have prevailed if they had depended on supply and demand conditions. However, as time went on the government responded to the pressure of producers by raising the fixed prices. Thus the official price for wheat in 1918 was two and a half times that fixed in 1915 when price control began.

The war brought an increased flow of money income to the peasantry both through the sale of the main crops at controlled prices and by the sale of other products which were subject to no control or only so far as sales to the army were concerned. Peasant families also received pay and allowances from their members who were mobilised. Middle-class consumers, accustomed to low prices at the expense of the peasantry, were outraged during, and more particularly after, the war, by what seemed to be the 'enrichment' of the peasantry. A new tension between town and country appeared. In a situation made complex by the great variety of conditions within the peasantry itself it is difficult to be sure how its material conditions were affected by the war. To begin with it made a heavy contribution in lives: 673,000 dead and another half a million seriously wounded.[8] Increased money incomes were matched by higher prices for the commodities which had to be bought. Undoubtedly, however, many families accumulated money reserves on a wholly new scale, permitting mortgages to be paid off and more land to be acquired. Moreover, the war tended to erase many of the old landmarks and heighten the expectations of the peasantry. Peasant soldiers were brought into contact with town life and standards. Army diet included meat, wine and other products on a scale few peasants had known before.

8. A total of 3·7 million agriculturalists were mobilised, *ibid.*, p. 115.

Whether higher money incomes represented a real or an illusory enrichment they profoundly affected the outlook and attitudes of the rural population, raising their aspirations and preparing the way for the intervention of the peasantry into political life in a way unknown before the war. As Augé-Laribé expressed it: 'Le paysan de 1914 est un resigné et celui de 1920 un mécontent.'[9]

IV

For all the upheaval and personal tragedy which it brought, the war left the agrarian structure fundamentally unchanged. The concentration of landed property was not greatly affected, no doubt in part due to the scarcity and relative high cost of hired labour which war losses intensified. For the rich there were other and more lucrative possibilities of adding to their wealth during the war than investment in land. Many farmers, *métayers* and peasants were only too anxious to purchase the land they tilled or to acquire more. Much of the new liquidity which found its way into their hands was thus passed on to those bourgeois and other landowners who sold off some or all of their holdings to the land-hungry peasants. In fact the peasantry not only survived the war but it was in some ways strengthened. Many of its members were able to make the best of the sellers' market which existed during the war and for some time afterwards. They became more keenly aware of money values and more able to strike a hard bargain. Thus the resentment of the urban petty bourgeoisie and newspaper readers, used to a docile peasantry and low prices. However, if large sections of the peasantry were now drawn more closely into an exchange economy than ever before, that meant exposure to the vicissitudes of the market. In

9. Augé-Laribé, *La Politique agricole* ..., p. 371. Although in his earlier book (Augé-Laribé and Pinot, *op. cit.*) on agriculture in wartime Augé-Laribé says, 'If anyone profited by the war it was not the French agriculturalist', nevertheless in his 1950 book, writing of the peasant in 1920, he states 'Sa situation materielle est cependant bien ameliorée. Il mange beaucoup plus de viande, il boit beaucoup plus de vin, sa nourriture est plus variée, le café est en permanence sur un coin du fourneau; il est mieux habillé, c'est à dire habillé comme un ouvrier de ville, avec une casquette et des chaussures de cuir. Tout cela ne le content pas. Il compare avec ce qui lui paraît mieux chez les autres. Il a appris à se plaindre' (p. 372).

fact, therefore, a new phase in the agrarian crisis began, however much, for the time being, it might be concealed behind a façade of prosperity.

The restoration of agriculture in the areas which were occupied or turned into battlefields during the war was one of the major tasks of reconstruction. While the state undertook the financial costs of reconstruction, as far as possible the physical tasks were left in the hands of private enterprise. Those who had lost real or personal property were compensated with 'war claims' which had to be spent within a radius of 50 kilometres of their former residence. Some of these claims were bought up by speculators for cash and then used to acquire land, usually for non-agricultural purposes.[10] The whole reconstruction programme was characterised by bureaucratic delays and by the unwillingness of the politicians to intervene in the agrarian sector with a positive programme of reform. On the whole reconstruction meant simply restoring the devastated regions as near as possible to their former state. However, under a law of 1919 some 600,000 hectares of land was reapportioned to give its owners compact plots.[11] Despite delays and abuses and the initial hardships of those who returned to the devastated areas—these included what had been some of the richest agricultural land—most of the area was restored to production within a few years.

French agriculture entered the postwar period under a conservative bourgeois government, helped to power by peasant votes, which was committed to restore as quickly and as fully as possible the free working of market forces. Politicians were always ready to launch into a eulogy of peasant virtues or to speak about the agrarian vocation of France, but were sparing in their support for positive measures of policy to give some substance to their words. There was, through the 1920s, no agrarian policy worthy of

10. Augé-Laribé calls it 'a traffic scandalous by reason of the profits accruing to these vultures of the battlefield, of the public spectacle of a just law frustrated of its purpose, and of the deplorable social consequences which may be foreseen. For these war claims bought from the peasants do not as a rule pass into the hands of agriculturalists. The speculators are manufacturers or businessmen who employ the indemnities to build factories or town houses to let', *Agriculture ... in France during the War*, p. 126. Just another of the minor public scandals which added to the disrepute of the Third Republic.

11. P. Barral, *Les Agrariens français de Méline à Pisani*, Paris, 1968, p. 199.

the term. Even the measures which were taken to assist cultivators to improve their methods met with resistance or indifference. A law of 1920 gave government support to agricultural credit institutions, extending their loans in the next decade. Nothing effective was done to deal with the problem of *morcellement* and a comprehensive programme for state technical aid put forward in 1927 fell victim to the economy drive and was only carried into effect in a truncated form.

The upward price trend inherited from the war was interrupted in 1920–21 and resumed again until 1926. Home market prices were kept down by the continuation of certain prohibitions on the export of agricultural products which had been imposed during the war, and perhaps by tariff rates which spokesmen for agrarian interests claimed had become too modest. Certainly French agriculture did not develop the export trade, as it might have done during this period. On the other hand, the home market was insulated to a considerable extent from world price trends. There was neither a determined policy to protect agriculture more adequately nor any desire to lower trade barriers to permit France to participate more fully in the international division of labour, with all the disrupting effects on the agrarian sector which would have resulted. Policy remained short-term, empirical and inconsistent. Determined by the big industrial and financial interests of the bourgeoisie concerned with business profits and reluctant to take measures which might accelerate still further the rising cost-of-living, it left things more or less as they were. Agriculture enjoyed a modest prosperity, a prosperity of the sort which benefited most those of the peasantry who were already better off. That many were dissatisfied with the standard of living offered by agriculture was shown by the continued drift from the land during the twenties.

If the twenties were moderately prosperous, the improvement in the agrarian sector was less than that in urban business. Industrial prices rose more than agricultural prices. The agriculturalist who compared his income, his standard of living and prospects with those of the townsmen might very well feel that he was not getting his due. The indifference or worse of the politicians and urban public opinion fed a growing sense of grievance in the villages. In some regions sections of the peasantry turned to the working class parties. There was an extension of peasant organisation, mainly along traditional and corporative lines, intended more to preserve existing positions than to demand big changes. The principal 'peasant' organisations on a national scale were not led by peasants at all. One was under the control of landowners and curés, the other of opportunist republican politicians drawn from the middle class.[12] Only in the 'thirties did more authentic peasant spokesmen begin to emerge.

V

Spared at first by its relative insulation from the world market from the effects of the price slide which followed the onset of the great depression in 1929, French agriculture began to be seriously affected from 1931. Prices fell drastically, surpluses piled up and peasant incomes were cut. For a time the peasantry began to make its voice heard as an autonomous and organised force. In any case, still making up approximately one-third of the population, it conserved a social weight which politicians ignored at their peril. If the peasantry stirred from its lethargy, legislators also shook off some of the inertia they had hitherto displayed towards the concerns of the agrarian community.

In examining the effects of the depression it is necessary to take note of certain peculiarities of French agriculture. First, with the exception of wine, it was almost entirely concerned with supplying the home market, not the world market. It was domestic purchasing power which provided the key to its fortunes. At the same time, seeing the staggering overproduction prevailing in the rest of the world the protectionist reaction to the crisis was extremely strong, it might be said instinctive. Secondly, being largely a peasant agriculture, still producing partly for subsistence, it could retrench on the basis of a lower income from cash crops and thus a curtailment of purchases of industrial goods. The rural exodus was arrested or even reversed as family

12. *Ibid.* 105–16.

members came back to find a security on the peasant holding which urban employment no longer offered.[13]

Despite the fall in world market prices in the first stages of depression, internal prices kept up fairly well until 1931–32—but existing levels of tariffs were not high enough to keep out a growing flood of cereals and other products from countries already suffering from overproduction. In the next few years agricultural surpluses began to pile up on French farms and storing them alone became a serious problem. Inevitably price levels came under pressure. By 1935 the price of wheat had fallen to about half of the 1929 level, that of wine to less than half.[14] The problem was intensified by good harvests at home. Higher tariffs, or tariffs raised more rapidly, might have had some effect in moderating the problem in the absence of any other solution within the confines of capitalism. Protection was resorted to, in any case, as the only way to handle the situation by the governments of the first half of the 'thirties. Reinforced with quotas and other administrative devices it curtailed the influx of cheap imports without relieving the plight of French agriculture, still beset by unsaleable surplus, falling prices and virtual insolvency. In the face of growing peasant discontent, politicians had reluctantly to accept that some measures of state intervention had become inevitable.

The watchword of policy thus became that of adapting production to the market.[15] This method was first adopted in 1931 to prevent the extension of the area under vine cultivation and was extended by the payment of bounties for reducing the area so used. In 1933 the attempt was made to fix a minimum price for wheat, and in the following year a bounty was paid for making surplus wheat unfit for human consumption. From 1935 the state bought up surpluses of wine, cider and beets for distillation into industrial alcohol. The effectiveness of such measures was reduced by evasions and exemptions. In the case of wine, the small growers who made up some two-thirds of the market were not included.

13. In 1911 40 per cent of the active male population was employed in agriculture; this had fallen to 35 per cent by 1926 and to 32·5 per cent in 1931, where it remained until after the Second World War. Barral, *Les Agrariens . . .*, Tableau IV, p. 217.
14. See Sauvy, *Hist. écon.*, ii, ch. 23, *passim*.
15. A good summary of these measures in *ibid*.

Sales of wheat below the minimum price were scarcely disguised. The apparatus did not yet exist to permit an effective control of production and marketing and unless producers saw an immediate material interest in the measures intended to stabilise prices they sought ways and means of evading them. At the end of 1934 the attempt to maintain a minimum price for wheat was abandoned in favour of the limitation of the sown area. The next harvest was 'fortunately' a bad one and the wheat price rose.

While the government took a series of piecemeal measures in their effort to stabilise agricultural prices output tended to increase. Since agricultural production was fragmented under the control of over six million cultivators who had been exhorted for years to improve their methods of husbandary this was not surprising. Many peasants responded to lower prices by increasing output in an attempt to maintain income. If restrictions were imposed on some sorts of production they turned naturally to others; wheat was fed to cattle or pigs with depressive effects on meat prices. Although *per capita* consumption of food tended to rise population was stagnant, or even fell slightly as immigrants left the country. The constricted market and the lower prices left the peasantry bearing a considerable part of the burden of the depression. Although both the Communist and the Socialist parties had a certain measure of support from the peasantry on a mainly localised basis, neither made much headway by offering a programme for a way out of the crisis. The vacuum was filled by right-wing demagogues of whom Henri Dorgères was the most successful.[16]

VI

The peculiarities of French capitalist development had led agriculture into an impasse. The preservation of a large peasantry, and thus of an overgrown agrarian sector of low efficiency, had largely been the result of the need of the bourgeoisie to ally itself with the peasantry against feudal-

16. His name 'was to become a symbol of barnyard demagoguery for a whole generation', G. Wright, *Rural Revolution in France* (Stanford, 1964), p. 50.

ism. But all parties, from the extreme royalist and clerical right to the Communist Party, courted the peasantry, each with their own type of demagogy. Although the politicians in Paris discounted the peasantry when it was relatively prosperous and thus quiescent, they competed for its electoral support when they needed it, and especially in a crisis like that of the 'thirties. Then they had to outbid each other with promises, if not with actual concessions. What these amounted to in practice was to leave things as far as possible as they were; to offer the peasants some protection against market forces while favouring most of all the highly organised interest groups, such as the beet-growers. The room for manoeuvre, and indeed for variation in the agrarian policy put forward to the rural electorate, differed comparatively little from right to left under such conditions. The supporters of liberal capitalism could not come forward openly with a programme which would mean the rapid concentration of holdings into larger, more efficient units and the proletarianisation of the peasantry on a mass scale. Nor could the parties of the left risk the loss of electoral support which would be entailed by presenting the need, with the necessary guarantees for the small peasant, for an immediate programme of cooperative and collective farming.

It was not surprising, in view of the inability of the parties in power to offer them any relief from the crisis, and the failure of the left-wing parties to convince the peasantry in the mass that they had a workable alternative, that tens of thousands of peasants turned in the 'thirties to new-style demagogues like Dorgères. The new saviours differed from the old mainly in that they were closer to the peasant masses, spoke their language and were not afraid to show their disrespect for the 'notables' and the old rural élite. But the remedies which the new agrarians proposed were no less backward-looking and conservative. They aimed to use peasant power to win concessions from government and so enable the peasant to keep control of his holding. They were opposed to structural change, whether taken to speed up industrialisation within a capitalist framework or as part of a socialist transition. Peasant grievances abounded and they made use of them, but the shallowness of the remedy was obvious enough. Enthusiasm for the new saviours proved ephemeral, but the stress on the rural virtues of a large property-holding peasantry was part of the mythology of the traditional right to which opportunist republican politicians also paid lip-service. What can be called 'peasantism' continued to flourish and came into its own, for a brief period, under the Vichy regime.

VII

It remains to see how the Popular Front approached the problems which its immediate predecessors had failed to grasp.[17] In fact, of the various projects for reform which were considered by Georges Monnet, the new Minister of Agriculture, only one of major importance was carried into practice, the setting up of the *Office du blé*.[18] The objective of the Blum government was to solve the crisis by raising purchasing power while placing the prices of agrarian produce on a more remunerative basis. The legislative project for the new organisation was introduced at once and became law in mid-August, 1936. The new organisation, whose full title was the *Office national interprofessionel du blé* (ONIB), was to take control of all dealings in wheat except for that required for household consumption, including imports and exports. In other words the Office bought the entire wheat harvest at a fixed price and became the source from which millers, bakers, exporters and manufacturers of food products obtained their supplies. Assisted by the fact that the subsequent harvests were below normal so that the Office had as much to do to moderate a price increase as to bring about a rise, its first two years of operation were mildly successful. In 1938 and 1939, owing to good harvests, the spectre of overproduction again arose and a severe burden was placed on the Office.

The *Office du blé* was strenuously opposed by the big

17. For the policies of the Popular Front see Sauvy, *Hist. écon.*, ii, Barral *Les Agrariens* . . ., pp. 243–55, Lefranc, *Hist. du Front Populaire*, pp. 342–64, Wright, *op. cit.*, ch. 4, *passim*, the title of which, 'Abortive New Deal', summarises his view of its efforts in the agrarian field.
18. Lefranc, *Hist. du Front Populaire*, pp. 344–50.

agrarian interests which saw in it the first step towards large-scale state intervention in agricultural marketing. In fact, the Popular Front did not follow it up with other measures of a like kind despite some discussion of a Wine Office. By the time it collapsed it had, in fact, done little else for the agrarian sector and Monnet's remaining projects remained unfulfilled. Whether or not it was attributable to the Blum government, the period 1936–38 saw some improvement in the income of the peasantry.[19] However, average peasant income remained near its 1913 level on the eve of the Second World War.

The interwar period brought greater changes to French agriculture than any comparable period since the Revolution. Structurally speaking, however, it brought no change at all. The role of agriculture in the economy had continued to decline steadily but in 1939 as in 1913 its weight still remained excessive for an advanced industrial country and kept down its *per capita* income and its rate of growth. In short 'deagrarianisation' had not proceeded far enough; this must be considered an outstanding weakness of French capitalism at this time. Agriculture had gone through a certain process of adaptation to the changing conditions of production and consumption. Yields had increased as a result of the wider use of fertilisers and improvements in methods of cultivation. Further improvement continued to be held back by the small size and irrational layout of the mass of small and many of the medium-sized holdings. Producers had learned that an increasingly urban society wanted more meat, dairy produce and vegetables and that the demand for cereals was inelastic. The land cultivated for cereals had somewhat diminished, that under grass had slightly increased. A good deal of marginal land had gone out of cultivation. But the changes

19. In a calculation of peasant purchasing power made by J. Dessirier in *Revue d'économie politique*, liii, 1939, already cited (see note 4), Augé-Laribé claimed that it had fallen to 80 per cent of the 1913 level after the war and did not recover until 1925. As a result of the price slide it fell off to 86 per cent in 1931–2, went down to 77 per cent in 1934 and to 63 per cent in 1935; it then began to recover, reaching 82 per cent in 1936 and falling off again to recover to 81 per cent in 1939. See 'La Production agricole', pp. 1174–5. It should be pointed out that this is the total income of the peasant sector and did not preclude improvement in family and individual incomes making possible the material improvements noted by Augé-Laribé in his article on the 'Structure agricole' in the same volume of the *Revue d'économie politique,* see especially pp. 147–9.

were too small to have anything like a revolutionary character.

In short, French agriculture had experienced the shock of a devastating war and had recovered from its effects, enjoyed a period of mild prosperity and then been flung into its most severe crisis and emerged to face the challenge of a new war with its physiognomy basically unchanged. Some modernisation there had undoubtedly been, but the influence of the past was still deeply written into the structure of the agrarian economy and made it inflexible to change—or a factor of stability, to which all the conservative forces in French society clung. Changes in peasant mentality there had undoubtedly been, but the revolution of expectations was still incomplete. Every year thousands of members of peasant families continued to vote with their feet for the opportunities and amenities of urban living until the depression temporarily arrested the process. That many peasants felt they were getting less than their fair share of income and legislative attention was clear enough. The claim that the Republic had neglected the land and the people who lived on it was used with some effect by the government of Marshal Pétain. And while there was a great deal of truth in it, the alternative which Vichy proposed had no meaning for an industrial country in the twentieth century, except under the very special conditions of military defeat and economic prostration.

11

THE CLOSING STAGES
1937–39

I

What blocked French recovery in the mid-1930s was the
continued crisis of confidence in the bourgeoisie, exacerb-
ated by the 'great fear' of 1936 when the country seemed to
stand on the brink of revolution. Confidence could not be
restored unless there was the expectation that investment
would be both safe and profitable and that the value of the
franc was secure. The conditions for recovery were more
psychological than economic. No remedy for the depression
was acceptable which did not provide a social climate and a
government which gave property-owners adequate assur-
ance that revolutionary change was not imminent. In their
existing state of irrational nervousness even Léon Blum
seemed to be a dangerous revolutionary and devaluation a
threat to the social order. The heightening of international
tension in Europe which followed the rise of Nazi Germany
and the ominous example of Spain gave further grounds for
fear. In the restoration of confidence diplomatic policy and
rearmament had to play a part. In its closing years the
search for security drew the political leaders of the Third
Republic into ever closer dependence on Britain and, less
directly, the United States. At the same time, the rearma-

ment drive became the major factor in the economic situation, providing to some degree the conditions for profitable investment, especially in the more advanced industries, which had hitherto been lacking.

The break-up of the Popular Front and the establishment of a new style of government by Daladier and Reynaud in 1938 created the essential political basis for at least a partial restoration of confidence and the inauguration of new policies acceptable to investors and employers. As the fears generated by 1936 in the minds of the ruling and middle classes tended to fade—though they never did altogether—so the hopes the working class had placed in the Popular Front ebbed away. In place of the militant optimism of the strike wave came growing confusion and disillusionment. The decisive blow fell with the defeat suffered by the one-day general strike of 30 November 1938. With this the Daladier government established its authority. In the closing years of the Third Republic there were signs that the palsy which had gripped politicians and the ruling class as a whole throughout the depression was at last being thrown off. But the new determination came too late and was still not decided enough to turn the tide. The initiative remained with Hitler and the review of policy and strategy in France was still only in its early stages when the war came, and with it the beginning of the relapse which ended with military defeat, the inglorious Armistice of June 1940 and the eclipse of the Third Republic. It was the end of an era but one which, perhaps, in its very last stage showed the signs of a new one.

The history of the last years of peace falls into two parts. First, the transition period marked by the two governments of Camille Chautemps and the shortlived second government of Léon Blum.[1] This period, which came to an end in April 1938, marked the final death agonies of the Popular Front and prepared the way for the second with the formation of the Daladier government, a shift to the centre-right and a more authoritarian form of government using decree-

---

1. Chautemps became premier in June 1937—he had held the post twice before—in a government which lasted until January 1938. After a ministerial crisis he formed a new government, without the Socialists, which lasted for only two months. Léon Blum then formed a shortlived government (of twenty-six days) to be followed by the government of Edouard Daladier which lasted until March 1940.

laws to press through a wide-sweeping programme designed to reassure the bourgeoisie. The economic background to this shift in the political centre of gravity can be briefly depicted in terms of the business cycle. The tendency towards a picking up of economic activity discernible in 1937 was soon compromised by the effects of the relapse in the United States.[2] With costs and prices in other industrial countries tending to fall and those in France moving upwards the advantages of the 1936 devaluation were lost and others necessarily followed. The franc lost ground on the foreign exchanges while confidence was undermined by the worsening international situation dominated by the Spanish Civil War, which widened the splits between the Popular Front partners, and by Nazi Germany's continuing and unchecked assault on the Versailles system which threatened French security. The Daladier government gained strength from its handling of foreign affairs and benefited from the renewed upturn in the world economy which accompanied the arms race. These favourable conditions greatly assisted the carrying through of the government's new policies on the financial and economic front.

II

The fall of the first Blum government was not strictly speaking the end of the Popular Front since the ministry formed by Camille Chautemps to replace it was supported by the Communist Party as well as by the Socialists who participated in it, but it did mark the end of the 'Blum experiment'.[3] Blum's presence in the government as vice-premier did not prevent it from reversing in fundamental respects the policy he had tried to carry out. Above all there was a return to financial orthodoxy evidently required to reassure bankers and investors whose confidence was still suffering from the 'great fear' of 1936. But it was also assumed that employers would have to be assisted by permitting greater flexibility in the application of the forty-

2. The monthly index of industrial production rose until March 1937, declined until the autumn when it picked up again, to fall to a new low point in August 1938.
3. Chautemps was granted the special powers which the Senate had denied to Blum.

hour week law, thus enabling a production drive to be carried out in industry. The restoration of the authority of the *patronat* was a central issue in 1937–38. The Chautemps government, and its successors still more, thus had to make inroads into the concessions made to the working class and the trade unions under the pressure of the strikes of 1936.[4] These years were marked, therefore, by bitter industrial disputes, the disintegration of the Popular Front and, within a short time, by the disillusionment and demoralisation of the working class. The recovery which took place in the closing years of peace was inevitably accompanied by the alienation of the working class more and more from the government and the regime and a partial return to the situation in industry which prevailed before 1936.

The Chautemps government set about restoring the financial situation by assuming power to legislate by decree for a period of two months from 30 June to 30 August 1937. It then proceeded to increase taxes, postal charges and railway rates and to decrease some expenditure items in the budget. These measures were accompanied by the assumption by the government of the power to fix by decree the gold value of the franc without any upper or lower limit. This was followed by the devaluation of the franc and the revaluation of the gold reserves of the Bank of France, the proceeds of which were to be applied to a new fund to keep up the market price of government securities[5]. The franc was devalued in order to end speculation and to encourage French exports which were increasingly handicapped by rising costs. In fact the franc was now a floating currency, there being no upper or lower limit to its gold value. Its value was adjusted downwards in September and again in April 1938. This enabled exports to conserve a cost advantage which contributed to economic recovery.

The emphasis of the Chautemps government was on financial orthodoxy, not on economic measures; it offered no permanent solution to the crisis but merely a temporary stimulant. Even its attack on the forty-hour week was half-hearted. It set up a commission of enquiry on the subject

4. Chautemps, and even Daladier in his first months in office, proceeded very cautiously along this path.
5. Sauvy, *Hist. écon.*, ii, pp. 262–3.

whose members, while criticising the inflexibility imposed on industry by the limitation of hours, recommended only mild proposals to permit additional hours to be worked. As long as the government depended on Socialist participation it was bound to move cautiously in whittling down what was regarded by the working class as a major gain.

In the controversies about the performance of the French economy after 1936 the forty-hour week comes in for a major share of blame. It is claimed that it raised costs, created bottlenecks in the supply of skilled labour and greatly limited the growth in production.[6] With the growing needs of rearmament these drawbacks became still more apparent, causing further inelasticities in supply of labour and materials at all levels. The existence of the law, and the criticism of the inflexible way in which it was at first applied, can easily conceal the more fundamental problems of the French economy in these years.

The forty-hour law was disappointing to its advocates mainly because it did not lead to the disappearance of unemployment. In any case, under capitalism, it was bound to raise costs which, in general, would be passed on—as they certainly were in France at this time—in higher prices to industrial and private consumers. In that sense it aggravated inflationary tendencies. But the law was felt as a burden by industry in large part as a consequence of the previous neglect of investment in modernisation and the inadequate expenditure on apprenticeship and training of the work force in the depression. In the longer run the limitation of hours should have encouraged the substitution of machinery for labour and thus an increase in productivity. French capitalism, at this time, was in too poor a shape to take up the challenge in this way. The forty-hour week, the outcome of the strike wave which had shaken the *patronat* to its core and created a hatred of the Popular Front and the unions, was used by many as a convenient scapegoat. It is necessary to understand that it was not merely a technical question but one in which class passions were deeply engaged. For many employers and sections of the bourgeoisie the attack on the forty-hour week was a question of revenge, as much as the release of a brake on industry.

6. See the works of Sauvy, Marjolin, Asselin and Lefranc already cited.

And, while economists and technicians see it in terms of industrial production and national welfare, this was hardly the way in which it presented itself to either side in industry.[7]

Given the parlous state to which French industry had been reduced, and especially with class tensions at breaking point, the limitation of the working week could only aggravate its problems. As a blanket measure it reduced the hours of work of all industrial personnel uniformly. However, skilled workers and technicians, because of the deficiencies in management in the past, were in short supply. Labour scarcities and bottlenecks of all kinds resulted. The unemployed could not fill the gaps created by the limitation of hours. The main result, therefore, was the continued stagnation of industrial production. It is difficult to see how, within the framework of capitalism, and given the relationship of social forces, there could be any other outcome. Of course, the attack on the forty-hour week was a constant theme of the press and politicians in all formations to the right of the Socialist Party, that is, including erstwhile supporters of the Popular Front. The hostility to it on the right reached a frenzy. In the closing period of the Third Republic one of the main preoccupations of the parliament elected in 1936 was to find a way to restore flexibility in the hours which could be legally worked in industry. This was the issue on which the last confrontation between the bourgeois state and the working class took place.

III

The working class were stubborn in their resistance to any increase in the legal working week and the unions made it as difficult as possible for exceptions to be made. The employers and their advocates blamed the law for a malady whose roots lay much deeper. They were asking the working class to make a sacrifice of time and leisure while condoning speculation, tax evasion, hoarding, disinvestment and the other practices blatantly indulged in by the

7. For a commonly accepted judgment see, for example, J. Néré, *La Troisième République, 1914–1940* (Paris, 1967), p. 148.

bourgeoisie and middle class. The attack on the forty-hour week is one-sided if it is abstracted from the whole social crisis of France at this time. It was not this one law which was responsible for the slow recovery of production or for the difficulties encountered by rearmament any more than the failure to establish exchange control was the exclusive reason for the disappointing results achieved by the successive devaluations of the franc after 1936.

In the short run the forty-hour week acted as a constraint on industry by limiting output because after a certain point rising costs eat deeply into profit margins. Those industries in which labour was scarce soon reached a ceiling and the limitations on their expansion were communicated to other industries in which the hours worked might remain below the legal maximum. This sort of inflexibility was pointed out by technicians and economists and it became clearer still as the rearmament drive began to have its effects. The industries most directly affected—steel, engineering, motors and aviation—were those most dependent on skilled labour which was in short supply. It was pointed out, therefore, that French rearmament was placed at a severe disadvantage compared with Nazi Germany where longer hours were worked and night work and shift working were general. It can be said, on the other side, that the past deficiencies of industry were now making themselves felt. Firms which had neglected investment in modern machinery and machine tools could only increase production by increasing the hours of work. The working class was therefore asked to give up what seemed to many to be the most substantial gain made in 1936. Hence the stubbornness of the resistance.

As long as the Popular Front coalition retained some semblance of unity and supported the government there could be no question of a serious inroad being made on the forty-hour week. It was in the second phase of the period 1937–39, after the fall of Chautemps, that the attack on the forty-hour week began in earnest. Until then the main priority was given to budgetary and monetary questions.

IV

The adoption of the floating franc shielded the economy to some extent from the American recession of 1937 and for a time industrial production rose. The main problem now seemed to be how to contain inflation. Rising prices ate into the increase in wages secured by the Matignon Agreement of 1936 and fed successive waves of industrial militancy. Although there was the beginning of a renewed confidence in financial and industrial circles, the Chautemps government remained tainted by its association with the Popular Front. Its life coincided with the assimilation of the forty-hour week by industry and then, after the upturn of 1937, the renewed decline in economic activity in the first months of 1938 associated with the US recession. Both the first Chautemps government and its revamped version without the Socialists were bounded by a desire to restore financial stability and a hesitancy in grasping the main problems—i.e. the making of serious inroads into the concession granted to the working class in 1936 and the gearing of the economy to the needs of rearmament and preparation for war.

The Chautemps government failed in its main aim: to restore the financial situation. Faced with a growing balance of payments problem, a budgetary deficit and growing agitation for higher wages to meet the rise in the cost of living the coalition began to fall apart. In January the Communist Party voted against the government and the Socialists withdrew their ministers from the cabinet. Persuaded to return to office a cabinet was formed again by Chautemps, this time without Socialist participation. It lasted barely two months, its fall coinciding with the Austrian crisis. It was followed by a shortlived ministry of twenty-six days headed by Léon Blum and accompanied by a renewed wave of strikes. The new government proposed to deal with the situation with new financial measures, notably a tax on capital and exchange control, but it was outvoted in the Senate and resigned. The Daladier government which replaced it in April 1938 marked an important step to the right and a more decided shift away from the policies of 1936 than Chautemps had been able to make.[8]

V

The new government, like its predecessor, placed its initial emphasis on a restoration of confidence through financial measures carried through by decree laws which did not have to be considered or passed by parliament. In face of the rising threat from across the Rhine rearmament became a dominant factor in the economic situation. The government was obliged to find ways of financing the rising arms budget without impairing the money or the willingness of investors to lend to the state. Vigorous measures were required, and taken, by a government which, because it leant increasingly towards the right, received the support and confidence of wider sections of the upper bourgeoisie and the middle class. The re-establishment of the authority of the state was necessary for the re-establishment of the authority of management in industry. The government thus moved towards an open confrontation with the working class culminating in the strike of 30 November 1938.

Thus, in 1938, a new style of government was inaugurated, accepted all the more readily because of the growing external dangers. However, economic difficulties following on the recession continued. The government therefore had to grapple with a difficult financial and economic situation on the basis of emergency measures designed for the short term. The budget deficit, open or concealed, continued to grow and was met principally by advances from the Bank of France. Gold continued to leave the country to seek refuge in the United States or some other haven as the risks of war increased. To meet this situation Daladier announced a new devaluation early in May 1938, linking the franc not to gold but to the pound sterling at not more than 179 to the pound.[9] In the following month the Bank of France was authorised to purchase short term government bonds on

8. Sauvy, *op. cit.*, does not rate Daladier any higher as an economist than Blum, but credits him with greater political sense; ch. 19 *passim.*

9. 'Pour la première fois, le franc était rattaché à une devise étrangère et non plus à l'or', Neurisse, *op. cit.*, p. 82.

the open market without limit. This method of financing a deficit attracted less attention than the usual one of direct advances to the state through the purchase of securities. It was more readily accepted by the investing public and enabled the government to finance its needs without undermining confidence in the franc. This resort to 'open market operations' was, in fact, a step on the road to war budgeting and in large measure was made necessary by the rising cost of armaments. Later in the year the reserves of the Bank of France were revalued and the advances to the state were reduced from the proceeds.

The Daladier devaluation was carried out as part of a determined policy to restore the authority of the state, to boost the confidence of the property-owning classes and re-establish the public finances on a sound basis. It was accompanied by a series of decree laws initiating a more vigorous policy in many economic and financial fields. The impression was given that at last there was a government which was in control of the situation and knew where it was going. At the same time, devaluation once again gave the export industries the possibility of contributing to recovery.

There remained the question of increasing national output and making room for the arms programme without reducing civilian production. It was assumed that the key to this problem lay in increasing the working week and therefore in abrogating the forty-hour week. This was the position taken up by Daladier and especially by Paul Reynaud who became Minister of Finance at the beginning of November. A long-time advocate of devaluation when it was a most unpopular cause and now an equally strong advocate of rearmament, Reynaud, in six years of opposition, had been a persistent critic of the weaknesses and failures of his predecessors. In his new role he was able to secure a wide measure of support—though the attack on the forty-hour week caused misgivings even in the cabinet itself because of the social dangers it seemed to raise. However, Daladier and Reynaud were convinced that if French capitalism were to be saved and if it were to survive in the dangerous international situation caused by the resurgence of Germany there had to be a break with the financial facility and the social concessions of the past. But to take back any of the 'conquests' made by the working class in 1936 led inevitably to a showdown. By November the government felt strong enough to undertake it.

The international situation continued to worsen with the threat to Czechoslovakia which resulted in a national emergency and partial mobilisation in September. The crisis was defused with the signature of the Munich agreement. What were the economic effects of this war crisis? As the possibility of war became apparent there was an increased demand for money, partly to stock commodities expected to be in scarce supply and to an even greater extent to meet unknown war contingencies. The effect on the price level was thus moderate. At the same time, as in 1914, mobilisation disorganised the economy by removing heads of enterprises or key personnel. Despite the mobilisation of a million men unemployment did not disappear. The adverse effects on civilian activity were not compensated for by a sufficiently rapid expansion of the war economy. However, towards the end of the year industrial production rose and the accelerated rearmament which followed the alert of the Czech crisis must be accounted the major factor in this upturn.

VI

The delayed showdown with the unions now had to be decisively fought out. By a further series of decree laws issued in November, Daladier and his Minister of Finance, Reynaud, showed their determination to end what the latter called the 'week of two Sundays'. The decrees included a number of government economies including the suspension of certain public works in order to make way for rearmament. In addition revenue was to be increased through the raising of taxes. Some forty thousand employees of the railway system (which had recently passed under semi-public control) were to be made redundant. Such measures could not fail to provoke bitter opposition from the trade unions.[10] Still more provocative were the measures an-

10. Reynaud announced these measures provocatively in a radio broadcast on 12 November, just before the opening of the Congress of the CGT at Nantes.

nounced to extend the working week beyond the legal forty hours established in 1936.[11] The contents of the decrees on hours of work were complex. They permitted extra hours to be worked to make up lost time or to cope with a sudden increase in orders. In the former case the *Inspecteur du Travail* had simply to be informed, in the latter his authorisation was required. In general, and throughout industry, these provisions made it possible, with little formality, to stretch the working day to nine hours, or forty-eight per week, and to re-establish Saturday working. Decrees issued relating to establishments working on national defence orders made possible further extension of hours, limited the payment for overtime, excluded certain questions from collective bargains and imposed penalties on workers who refused overtime.

Meeting at Nantes soon after the publication of the decree laws the Congress of the Confédération Générale du Travail manifested its hostility and called for 'a national day of protest'.[12] But the demand for something more than that was made by many constituent unions and by workers in the factories. It was therefore decided to call a one-day general strike for 30 November. The government determined to make this a test case of its authority. It presented the strike as a political strike and the prelude to insurrection, thus ensuring the support of the middle class for the measures it proceeded to take. Wide publicity was given to these measures in order to reduce support for the strike as far as possible. Public servants were requisitioned in their jobs. Considerable police forces were brought into Paris and the main industrial centres, backed up by troops. Despite the wide support which the strike call received in many industries, in the coal mines and in building, it proved to be a decisive victory for the government, a kind of revenge for

11. A specialist commentator claimed that the struggle to maintain the forty-hour week in its integrity dominated the thought of the union leaders at this time. 'L'-affaire des 40 heures semblait devenir pour la CGT une question d'amour-propre, qu'elle défendait avec une sorte de passion sourde à tous les raisonnements, aveugle à toutes les réalités économiques', 'Le Marché du travail et le mouvement syndical' in *Revue d'économie politique*, liii, mai-août, 1939, p. 1354. The article explains the changes in the law. It is not difficult to see that it was pressure from the rank and file which obliged the union leaders to adopt an intransigent position. But the Jouhaux wing did not relish strike action.
12. Lefranc, *Le Mouvement Syndical*, pp. 382–5.

May-June 1936. Many strikers in the public services were sacked, others in private industry were victimised. The failure of the strike carried forward the process of disillusionment in the working class which had been going on for some time. Trade union membership fell away sharply as did the support for the Socialist and Communist parties. An enormous blow had been struck at the moral authority of the trade union leaders whether supporters of Jouhaux or of the Communist Party, already undermined by the events of 1937 and the series of unsuccessful strikes in 1938.[13]

The defeat of the strike gave the government the authority and prestige which it sought and did more than anything else to restore confidence.[14] Capital was repatriated, the franc appreciated to 177 to the pound, share prices rose and the rate of interest fell. By the end of 1938 solid progress appeared to have been made, especially in the financial and monetary spheres. In the economic field the conditions had been established for a measure of recovery.[15] Assisted by the powerful stimulant of rearmament undertaken in an atmosphere of liberalisation deliberately created by the Daladier–Reynaud government, and now without the strait-jacket of the forty-hour week, an industrial revival began. To some extent, at least, profitability had been restored both in the home market by rearmament and in the world market by devaluation. Meanwhile, again in the short run, the economy benefited by the growing fears of war in Europe and the menace of German expansion. Not only did French capitalists repatriate part of their holdings sent

13. For developments in the working class movement, see the article by Broué and Dorey already cited.
14. As an economist reported: 'L'insuccès total de la grève générale du 30 novembre, en consacrant, d'une façon incontestable, la désagrégation de la formation politique qui était au pouvoir depuis juin 1936, a agi puissamment sur l'esprit public et sur la confiance des épargnants et des milieux commerciaux ou industriels. Les résultats escomptés des dernières mesures de redressement financier ont provoqué un retour accéléré des capitaux exportés et une liquidation complète des anciennes positions à la hausse sur les devises étrangères.'—'Le Marché monétaire' by P. R. in *La Revue d'économie politique*, liii, 1939, 1017.
15. Another contributor to *La Revue d'économie politique*, writing about the stock exchange, now saw France definitely on the road to recovery thanks to the return to 'serious methods of government'—'le redressement général, amorcé en 1938, se poursuit vigoureusement, avec des résultats presque inespérés dans le domaine financier et monétaire, à un rythme encore trop lent dans le domaine économique, en raison de la réadaptation délicate qui s'impose, compte tenu de la politique de surarmement', J. Dessirier, 'La Bourse des Valeurs', pp. 1097–8.

abroad for safety in 1936–37, but some foreign capital now took refuge in Paris. The reserves of the Bank of France reflected the swing.

The economic situation in 1939 was increasingly dominated by rearmament. The working week was further prolonged in factories working on defence orders. The revival was thus most apparent in the war industries, while in other fields the stagnation continued. There was far from being a strong and generalised recovery and some part of the improvement was found to be of a mainly short-term character. The measures taken by the Daladier–Reynaud government could not, in the short run, overcome the deep-seated weaknesses of French capitalism. Indeed, the needs of rearmament in some cases merely exposed these weaknesses: inadequate mechanisation, lack of raw material supplies, scarcity of skilled labour. The basis for a large-scale arms programme had largely to be created after eight or nine years of industrial rundown. The longer working week was not sufficient to enable the deficiencies of the past to be made good. Moreover, industrialists continued to be cautious about increasing investment and expanding output; restrictionism died hard even under the impetus of rearmament.

By the outbreak of war in September 1939, then, French recovery, already so belated, remained partial and uneven. Would it have taken place at all without armaments spending? The answer remains in dispute but the fact was that the international situation demanded that France should join the arms race. The immediate problem was that she did so under serious handicaps compared with other countries. The industrial decline had gone a long way by the time that rearmament became effective. French industrial potential was not such that it could cope, within the space of a few years, with the massive needs of a modern war economy. Nor was there time, before the outbreak of war, to carry through the necessary programme of industrial re-equipment and modernisation. And, although part of the arms industry was brought under state control, private entrepreneurs hesitated to make the necessary outlays, or still lacked confidence in the regime and in the future. The government was not anxious to extend the area of economic controls: its policy rested, somewhat paradoxically, on a combination of economic liberalism and orthodoxy with a drive to restore the authority of the state. Above all, from the military point of view, the preparations being made were for the war which was expected and not the war of movement, based on armoured divisions and aerial support, which actually took place in 1940.

VII

Despite the signs of a recovery in 1938 under the stimulus of the approaching war, the balance sheet of the previous decade was a dismal one. There had been a serious regression in the absolute as well as the relative position of French capitalism. Its crisis had been deep and prolonged and it was still not over: the plunge into war and the suddenness of the defeat were to extend it and bring it to a climax. Since 1929 the active population had fallen from 21·9 million to 20·4 million. The consumption of energy had fallen by 13 per cent on a *per capita* basis, although the consumption of electricity had increased. Industrial production as a whole was only about 86 per cent of what it had been before the slump.[16] Of the major branches of industry only paper, rubber, gas and electricity produced more than in 1929; the performance of iron and steel (64 per cent), of building (61 per cent) and of leather (72 per cent) were especially dismal. Investment had slowed and in some instances had come to a standstill; consequently the age of machinery and machine tools in use had lengthened.[17] French industry was becoming increasingly obsolescent. The iron and steel industry, a brilliant performer of the 1920s, had fallen back and production per man year had dropped by nearly 20 per cent.[18] When rearmament began

16. Most of these statistics are to be found in the Appendices to Sauvy.
17. Thus the average age of machine tools at the end of the Second World War was stated to be twenty-five years in France against six or seven in the United States and Russia and seven to nine in Britain. See J. Fourastié and H. Montet, *L' Économie française dans le monde* Paris, 1946.
18. From 64·6 tons to 48 tons; see D. S. Landes, *The Unbound Prometheus* Cambridge, 1969, p. 479. He quotes a report of the *Institut National de la Statistique et des Études Économiques* which states that on the eve of the war 'French metallurgical plant was in a state of profound obsolescence', p. 478.

in earnest, in some plants tanks had to be made almost with nothing but files and hammers.[19]

France's underindustrialisation, which even some economists who should have known better described as a 'balanced' economy, had the effect of shielding her from some of the worst effects of the slump. As has been pointed out, unemployment was a less severe problem than in more highly industrialised countries. In 1938 France had fewer unemployed drawing relief than Nazi Germany, which was supposed to have overcome unemployment through arms spending, a fifth as many as in Great Britain and only slightly more than in the Netherlands.[20] The fact that some 30 per cent of the active population was 'employed' in agriculture—really underemployed and perhaps idle for a good part of the year—was not foreign to this apparently happy situation. But French agriculture, if judged by yields of cereals and potatoes, was still the least efficient in western Europe.[21] Despite restriction schemes total agricultural output was a per cent or two up on 1929. The anachronistic French peasantry, despite low prices, tried to produce more in an effort to maintain its incomes. Meanwhile the value of the franc had taken further severe blows and its purchasing power had fallen by more than 60 per cent compared with 1929. All in all, disregarding the variations in the standard of living of different classes and sections of classes, France was a poorer country by over 10 per cent, the amount by which production per head had fallen compared with 1929. So recovery still had a long way to go even to catch up with the performance of 1929.

19. 'En fait, on n'a trouvé dans certaines industries que des limes et des marteaux pour fabriquer des chars d'assaut' said a former Conseiller d'État who took part in the colloquium on Léon Blum, *op. cit.*, p. 291.
20. Sauvy, *op. cit.*, p. 554.
21. Wheat output was 15·3 quintals to the hectare against 29·5 in the Netherlands, 22·8 in Britain and 22·1 in Germany; potatoes yielded 108 quintals per hectare against 178 in the Netherlands, 168 in Britain and 164 in Germany. Sauvy *op. cit.*, p. 541.

12

THE BALANCE SHEET
OF A DECLINE

I

To draw up a balance sheet of the development of French capitalism in the period 1913 to 1939 is a complex task to which it is hoped that the preceding chapters will have contributed. It remains to bring together what seem to be the main conclusions of this study, recognising their provisional nature. The first of these, and not open to question, is that on the international or the European plane France had declined relatively over this period. This was clearly in part an inevitable decline. The rise of American economic power, the economic upsurge of Russia and Japan and the spread of industrialisation to new areas of the world made this a process in which the whole of western Europe shared and to which the waste of life and destruction of resources during the First World War made an indubitable contribution. It may be said, in any case, that the resources did not exist in France to make possible the economic strength which could have prevented a relative decline. The rise of industrial Germany in the second half of the nineteenth century, the defeat suffered by France in the war of 1870–71, showed that European hegemony had slipped beyond her grasp. The position France held in

Versailles Europe, with the temporary eclipse of Germany, could not last. The balance of economic forces tilted inevitably against French capitalism, weakened, as it was in so many ways, by the war.

Victory in the First World War was made possible only by the support France received from the Anglo-American powers. But victory was achieved at the price of tremendous sacrifices, especially disproportionate, compared with her allies, as far as the loss of life was concerned. Hence the resentment which built up after the signature of the Treaty of Versailles because the Anglo-Americans did not insist on making Germany pay reparations and regarded with suspicion, rather than with approval, the attempt of French governments to establish the pre-eminence of their country in European power politics and to keep Germany disarmed and weak. The French ruling class was now faced with dangers which had not been present at all before 1914. The Bolshevik Revolution, together with the growth in the size of the working class at home and the impact on it of that Revolution, raised the threat of a struggle for power in a more immediate way than at any time since the Commune. Fortunately for the French ruling class this threat, in the first postwar years, was never as serious as in Germany and Central Europe. It was not until the 'thirties that it again raised its head; but the fear was there. On a different plane, but one of no less concern to the bourgeoisie, France entered the postwar years plagued by currency instability—a wholly new and extremely disturbing phenomenon which, with the interlude of the *franc Poincaré*, was to continue throughout the interwar period.

Despite currency disorder and its social consequences, French industry in the 'twenties progressed and prospered. This was partly due to the energy and rapidity with which reconstruction was carried out, despite the failure to obtain the expected reparations from Germany, partly to the favourable international conjuncture of the 'twenties. During the war and the postwar years industrialisation was carried forward in old and new industrial regions. Whole industries were modernised and re-equipped and industry spread to some places for the first time in the special wartime conditions. New battalions were added to the ranks of the industrial proletariat from the rural population and also, to the extent of some three million, from immigration. While the proletariat remained a minority, its specific weight had increased and it consisted, to a large extent, of a new, raw and heterogeneous mass not tightly controlled by a traditional reformist trade union apparatus and political machine.

But while the war and its aftermath saw a strengthening of the proletariat in numbers, it saw a weakening in sections of the large middle class with which French society was endowed. It was not that these sections declined in size but that they suffered material or moral losses as a result of the war and the social change accompanying industrialisation. Even when such losses were not quantitatively measurable in terms of income or wealth and may, indeed, not have existed, they were believed to exist. So many of the old landmarks and certainties had been swept away in the cataclysm that there was an undoubted sense of loss and deprivation. There were, however, real losses for some: holders of bonds of the Russian and other defaulting governments; those on fixed incomes in a period of inflation; owners of house property subject to rigid rent controls imposed during the war; artisans unable to compete with factory industries; small businessmen who lost out in the competitive struggle.

If the war imparted a new dynamic to the economy this was not fully understood at the time. Masses of Frenchmen of the middle class were more frightened by inflation, budgetary disorder and the depreciation of the franc than they were encouraged by the evidence of industrial revival. The peasantry had its own grievances, for, after a period of 'enrichment' more illusory than real, agricultural incomes failed to regain their pre-1913 level in real terms. Affected with the peasantry were sections of the artisan and small commodity producers, dealers and shopkeepers who made up the population of the small towns which dotted the French rural landscape. Every step which the economy made towards modernisation and further industrialisation undermined the livelihood, reduced the income and intensified the feeling of insecurity of many in these categories. As was to be expected they declined over the period in absolute numbers: from the point of view of equipping French capitalism to face the competitive rigours of the twentieth century they did not decline fast enough. They embodied and personified the archaisms and structural rigidities which stood in the way of faster growth and higher *per capita* income.

It is obviously difficult to establish how much weight should be attached to the demographic factor in accounting for France's economic difficulties in the interwar years. The fact is that notwithstanding the return of Alsace-Lorraine, as well as large-scale immigration, the population in 1936 was only larger by 1 per cent than in 1911. During that period it had aged perceptibly, the proportion of under-twenties falling from 34 to 31 per cent while the over-sixties had risen from 12 to 14 per cent. Not until the 1930s were measures taken, notably through family allowances, to deal with a falling birth rate which seemed to threaten the country with depopulation in the latter part of the century.

The labour scarcity was made good by large-scale immigration and since, at least at first, the immigrants had larger families than the native-born, they helped to counteract the declining tendency in the birth rate. Therefore, it can hardly be said that the economic stagnation was directly connected with labour scarcity or high wages resulting from such scarcity. However, the demographic pattern affected the shape and rate of growth of market demand and un-consciously influenced investment decisions and public policy. It tended to confirm French businessmen in their caution and routinism by suggesting that there was a more or less fixed demand, the main thing being to secure a share of this market. When overproduction arose it was aggrav-ated by the stagnation in market growth, the missing con-sumers who had not appeared because of millions of decisions to restrict family size. For agriculture, which was uncompetitive on world markets, this was particularly serious. Both in agriculture and in industry the response to the situation was restrictionism, or what the French called 'Malthusianism' by analogy with the limitation of popula-tion.

Restrictionism in the 'thirties was far from being specific

to France. But it can be held that business and the state carried it to extreme and self-defeating lengths and that the reason for this was connected with the demographic situation. It represented a lack of confidence in the future which went with the ageing of the population; it made for a short-term view—to hang on to what had been acquired rather than taking risks in order to secure larger but uncertain returns in the future. It drained away the sources of enterprise and energy in the bourgeoisie and made even Paul Reynaud declare at one stage: 'It seems to be contemplating its own funeral.'

The restrictionist mentality was dominant in every field of private and public decision-making and was intensified as a result of the depression. Agricultural policy was based on insulating the producer still more from the foreign market, curtailing the cultivated area and destroying or denaturing food products. Industry responded likewise by limiting production, cutting back on investment and innovation, while seeking ways to maintain prices and divide up the market among the existing producers. Organised economic interests sought government support to back up such measures with considerable success.[1] While lip-service was paid to the virtues of economic liberalism, increasingly, in the 'thirties, the free market became a regulated market designed to conserve the positions of those already in possession. The measures taken to limit the growth of modern forms of distribution such as chain stores provide an excellent example of how 'Malthusianism' encouraged inefficiency.

II

The restoration of the franc by Poincaré seemed to be the signal economic success of the decade of the 'twenties. It restored confidence while giving French exports a competitive edge which enabled them to take full advantage of the

1. Private interests literally 'besieged' the government to pass laws to defend the positions which they had acquired and to guarantee the incomes and profits to which they considered they were entitled. An outline is to be found in W. C. Baum, *The French Economy and the State* (Princeton, 1958), which deals, however, mainly with the immediate post-1945 period.

closing stages of the boom and to ward off, for two to three years, the full impact of the world economic depression. For this brief period France seemed to be an island of prosperity in a crisis-stricken Europe. Once the crisis did strike its effects were no less damaging than in other countries, though the forms they took contained specifically French features. Unemployment, for example, though unprecedented by national experience, was not as heavy as in more highly industrialised countries. Nor was there mass impoverishment on the scale of other countries. The size of the peasantry and the continued family links of many urban-dwellers with the land provided a kind of cushion against unemployment. Some of France's unemployment was passed on to other countries by the return of immigrants. Artisans and small independent producers, like the peasants, simply retrenched, accepting lower money incomes and hoping for better days: though some became more corporatively self-conscious and militant as those days failed to arrive.

Once in the grip of depression the economy failed to generate forces making for recovery and entered on a prolonged stagnation which was intensified by the response of government and business alike. Both reflected a deep crisis of confidence in the bourgeois class in France as the old world which had nurtured it appeared to be disintegrating. In the face of the oncoming deluge the main watchword was survival; but even with this in mind the bourgeoisie stuck tenaciously to the methods of the past and treated all departures in policy or innovations in methods with suspicion or hostility. It was a class which seemed determined to accelerate its own doom.

In the new situation created by the world economic depression, and especially by the competitive exchange depreciation on which other countries embarked, addiction to the *franc Poincaré* was disastrous. But bourgeois opinion was unable to break with its old monetary prejudices; the gold value of the stabilised franc became taboo. Failing to understand the international character of the crisis, and particularly the importance of exports for industrial prosperity in France, policy-makers permitted French goods to be priced out of the bitterly competitive

167

world market of the 'thirties. They were supported by bankers and financiers and the whole weight of orthodox opinion. Together with the fetish of budgetary equilibrium the taboo of stable money inhibited governments from dealing with the depression by measures of reflation and expansion of the sort taken more or less empirically everywhere else. After being an island of prosperity in a sea of depression, France had to see her rivals undergo a measure of resurgence while she slipped further below the waters.

In the first half of the 'thirties French capitalism experienced to its cost the last determined attempt to employ deflation as a remedy for depression; the elementary lesson that such a policy could only make matters worse had to be learned the hard way. France became a laboratory experiment for proving what was soon to be obvious: that a country cannot get out of a depression by scrimping and screwing. But the grip of liberal economic orthodoxy and fear of currency instability and inflation were so powerful that the demonstration could not be avoided. The refusal to devalue made necessary budgetary stringency which raised opposition from many quarters and prepared the way for the electoral victory of the Popular Front of the left parties in May 1936. But despite the facts that some of its leaders had been converted to devaluation and that its policy rested on the aim of expanding purchasing power, it still did not come forward during the election as an advocate of devaluation. Nothing would have been more likely to ensure its defeat.

Malthusian policies dominated the response of business to the depression just as it did that of government. The more control industry had over the market through tariffs and monopoly the more it limited output in order to maintain prices and profitability.[2] Even in the most advanced industries, those which had been re-equipped and done well in the 'twenties, confidence in the future seemed to be replaced by despondency. New investment came to a stop. Innovation was regarded with suspicion. Management

2. Bettelheim, *op. cit.*, lays great emphasis on the growth of monopoly as a main factor accounting for the retrogression of the 1930s. Of course, monopoly capitalism was even more developed in other countries which did show signs of recovery, so this could not have been the decisive factor.

techniques fell behind. Apprentices were reduced in number. Profits were hoarded, invested outside the firm in short-term bonds and moved for safety abroad at the least hint of trouble, financial, political or social. French products fell out of the world market as they became uncompetitive in price and then in quality. French industrial equipment taken as a whole, much of which had been replaced in the

TABLE 3. *Industrial production (1952 = 100).*

Year	with building	without building
1928	83	84
1929	92	90
1930	92	88
1931	79	75
1932	68	64
1933	74	73
1934	69	68
1935	66	67
1936	71	73
1937	75	78
1938	69	72

Source: *Annuaire Statistique,* 1966.

TABLE 4. *Industrial production: annual average (1928 = 100)*

Year	General	Steel	Textiles	Building	Paper
1931	94	83	80	127	108
1932	78	58	74	99	104
1933	88	67	89	93	142
1934	82	63	78	85	160
1935	79	63	80	73	149
1936	85	68	86	70	178
1937	89	82	88	66	186
1938	83	64	84	61	154

Source: Sauvy, *op. cit.,* Table vii, 2, p. 532.

'twenties, now went through a process of moral deterioration. Like the population, the age of machines and machine tools increased and their technical level fell behind that in other countries where a genuine or stimulated industrial recovery had begun by 1933 or 1934.[3] French recovery was assisted neither by 'new' industries nor by any significant structural changes of the sort which signalised recovery and a resumption of transformation in Britain. Housing, under the influence of stagnant population and artificially low rents, remained a depressed sector. The market for domestic appliances, furniture and 'modern' consumer goods was affected in the same way. There was no great shift in demand to promote investment in such sectors.

Until the pull of rearmament began to make itself felt at the end of the 'thirties and successive devaluations had made French prices more competitive, industry stagnated well below the level of the late twenties (see Tables 3 and 4). Where concentration and monopoly had advanced most completely the giant firms used their power to restrict output and maintain prices and profits. The former vanguard industries of the postwar wave of industrialisation became as restrictionist and conservative as the rest. Firms preferred to accumulate liquid reserves rather than to invest and innovate. Banks, financial institutions and investors encouraged the trend. To make matters worse for the economy as a whole these liquid funds were volatile and internationally mobile. Part of the 'flight from the franc' was made up of capital which might otherwise have found its way into industrial expansion.

III

Judging from the behaviour of the large firms it seems contradictory to say that what much of French industry suffered from was excessive fragmentation and lack of coordination. Especially in the consumer goods industries such as textiles, established in the previous century, the

3. It was just at this time that an economist reported, with reference to machinery and machine tools, 'les achats de la clientèle nationale sont tombés à un niveau faible; si dans quelques cas plutôt exceptionnels, des usines ont jugé opportun de moderniser leur équipement en vue de comprimer leur prix de revient la plupart des entreprises hésitent, au contraire, à rénover ou à aggrandir leur parc de machines'. Nevertheless, he went on to add that despite tariffs, foreign machine imports were competing successfully with French products.—Henri Laufenburger, 'Les industries métallurgiques et méchaniques', *Rev. d'écon. pol.* xlix (1935), special number on 'La France économique en 1934', p. 861. See the articles on other industries in the same number, and also 'La production industrielle' by P. Jéremac.

old style family capitalism survived. Family firms conserved their identity with great tenacity in the face of contracting markets and shrinking profits. Their structure enabled them to do this since they did not depend on outside sources of capital and could retrench financially during the depression. When prices and profits fell workers were sacked or put on short-time and investment came virtually to an end. Family members took a cut in income or lived off capital, meanwhile keeping their reserves as liquid as possible and contributing to the movements of capital abroad. The consumer goods industries were severely affected by the depression, lost many of their foreign customers and suffered from the falling off of tourism.

Despite the constant complaints of the representatives of artisan and small-scale industry that they were being driven to the wall by the competition of large capitals, they displayed considerable capacity to survive.[4] Many artisan activities were closely tied to the preservation of a peasant agriculture and were carried on in the small towns which dotted provincial France.[5] But the important luxury and semi-luxury industries were also organised largely on a small scale and even gave much employment to one-man businesses or to workers in their own homes. Even advanced industries, such as motor-cars, found it advantageous to employ outworkers and small subcontractors for the supply

---

4. It is not easy to give statistical precision to the question. From one point of view concentration of production had been a main trend: a larger proportion of the working population was employed in large establishments while the number of small firms had declined. For instance, between 1926 and 1931 the numbers employed in establishments of from 1 to 5 workers had fallen from 832,496 to 740,010. On the other hand, the number of small firms and artisanal enterprises remained extremely large. In 1931 the breakdown of workers in manufacturing industry was as follows:

2,651,134 in units employing from 1 to 10
438,714 in units employing from 11 to 20
670,172 in units employing from 21 to 50
576,897 in units employing from 51 to 100
2,356,826 in units employing over 100

J. Denuc, 'Structure des entreprises', *Rev. d'écon pol.* liii (1939), p. 223.
5. Artisan industry is taken to be a form of production in which the owner of the enterprise executes the same tasks as his employees. This is the definition suggested by T. J. Markovitch in 'L'industrie française de 1789 à 1964—sources et méthodes', *Cahiers de L'I.S.E.A.*, no. 163 (July 1965), who points out that it still remains more widespread in France than is often assumed. Denuc, *op. cit.*, p. 222 gives the following figures based on the Census of 1931: 1,050,000 male small masters; 158,000 male domestic workers (*à façon à domicile*); 657,000 female small employers (*petites patronnes*); and 260,000 female domestic workers.

of such parts as carburettors. During the 1930s the effects of depression may have arrested the process of concentration; some workers employed by larger firms set up on their own as an alternative to unemployment. On the other hand there were complaints that social legislation was making it increasingly difficult for the smaller employer to stay in business.

If the way forward for the older sections of French industry still dominated by small firms seemed to lie in combination and concentration, the fields in which these tendencies had gone forward most rapidly hardly offered a brilliant example. In any case, the way of survival and expansion, which required mergers, takeovers and a transfusion of fresh enterprise, management and capital, was itself blocked by the prevailing social and economic climate. It was not until the 'fifties that conditions for a change began to ripen and even then the process was slow in developing. Down to the Second World War, therefore, French industry seemed to have the worst of both worlds. It demonstrated the worst traits of monopoly and restrictionism in large-scale industry side-by-side with the conservatism, routinism and timidity which characterised many of the old-style firms. There was much coexistence between them on the basis of live and let live. There were many industrial archaisms carried over from the nineteenth century. As long as it is remembered that France had had a large-scale modern industrial sector since the latter part of the nineteenth century which had shown its capabilities in the first postwar decade, certain of the strictures foreign observers made on French enterprise after the Second World War can be accepted.[6] But the old and the archaic had survived for complex reasons which cannot be explained from the nature of the entrepreneurs alone but involves an analysis of the whole environment which produced them.

Many forces contributed to this environment, as previous chapters have shown. They were bound together in an historically-conditioned structure which made up French

6. See the works by Landes, Cameron and others on the French entrepreneur cited page 10 note 2, which were influenced very much by the conditions which prevailed in the 1930s and immediately after the Second World War.

capitalism and distinguished it from the form this mode of production took in other geographical settings and where it had developed under different conditions. It is only by probing this totality of relationships that we can deepen our understanding of these peculiarities. No one factor, such as entrepreneurship, lack of natural resources, the demographic slowdown or even the preservation of a large peasant sector, suffices to explain the peculiarities of the economic structure and its proneness to stagnate for about a quarter of a century before, during and after the Second World War.

There was no cure for the ills of French capitalism in policy measures. More monopoly and concentration could hardly be seen as a remedy for the older, more backward sectors when it only meant restriction and the standstill of investment in the industries where these forms were most advanced. In the same way, successive governments pursued policies which tended to make the depression worse or, with the advent of the Popular Front, undermined confidence and did nothing to restore profitability. However, policy, both private and public, expressed the interests and understanding of those who took decisions. Politicians and businessmen were prisoners of a particular milieu, shared its prejudices and reflected its limitations. It is possible, with hindsight, to write a recovery programme for French capitalism which might, in theory, have lifted it out of the depression earlier. It would contain an early devaluation of the franc (from 1932), deficit financing and public works, and measures to aid industrial re-equipment and carry through the reorganisation of agriculture. Such an exercise would have no more than academic interest; it presupposes knowledge of Keynesian theories and techniques; and it assumes that they would have worked. In any case, there was no conceivable governmental combination ready to put forward such a programme and even if there had been politicians willing to support it they would have had no chance of obtaining power. The fate of Reynaud, the main public figure advocating devaluation, is eloquent in this regard. So is the timidity of the Popular Front when confronted with the necessity to carry forward a devaluation or to face a budget deficit. Even such an elementary measure as exchange control to deal with currency move-movements and speculation was regarded as out of the question and explicitly rejected.

IV

The problems lay too deep in French society and in its inherited structures to be treated at that time within the framework of capitalism. Most measures taken by the state tended to make them worse, and the bourgeoisie as a whole could do little more than hang on grimly to acquired positions without much confidence in the future of the system they represented. The threat of revolution, revealed in 1936, added to the paralysis and indecision, while the dramatic choices which had to be made in the international field, and the imminent threat of war, added to the division and confusion within the ruling class.

For practically a decade regression and stagnation characterised almost the whole of the economy. Even the impetus of rearmament was not sufficient to promote more than a partial and long delayed recovery. The comparative performance of French capitalism shows up as the worst among the advanced countries. The French crisis was a specific form of a general crisis affecting all the capitalist countries—it represented the inability of this mode of production to develop the productive forces within the old social relations. It led directly to the Second World War, which in turn, by a grim paradox, prepared the way for a more favourable conjuncture in which the French economy was once again able to expand. Under the hammer blows of the German *Blitzkrieg* French society was shattered and it was not until the 1950s that the pre-depression levels of production were achieved and as the result of structural changes which were imposed as the price of survival. The fact remains that the crisis in France was particularly prolonged and intense and led directly to military defeat and occupation. Why was this? A possible answer can be found in the archaisms preserved in the economic structure, namely a large contingent of still partly self-sufficient peasants with low purchasing power and small commodity producers representing the older forms of capitalism or even precapitalist structures. Thus French capitalism, when afflicted with the depression, was still incompletely transformed to meet the requirements of the twentieth century. Half-completed modernisation made public opinion and the social and economic structure inflexible to change: the stagnation appeared to have become permanent; any change could only undermine a precariously held equilibrium. In the French context, the rapid development of the productive forces, which had been the historical justification for capitalist property relations, had come to a halt.

It can hardly be contested that the economic decline of the interwar period prepared the way for, if it did not make inevitable, the military defeat which ended the life of the Third Republic. But while industrial shortcomings and stagnation may have influenced the quantity and quality of military equipment and the lack of preparedness for a total war, the completeness of the demoralisation and collapse of 1940 requires deeper explanations. It may be suggested that it is in the complex interaction of economic decline with the crisis of confidence of the bourgeoisie and its political representatives that the conditions for the débâcle were prepared. Industrialists, financiers, investors and politicians were swept by a wave of pessimism about their right to rule and their capacity to overcome the crisis their society was passing through which paralysed their will and made them incapable of formulating and carrying through a coherent policy. They appeared to be inescapably trapped between the dangers from within symbolised by the events of 1936 and the aggressive rivalry of the Third Reich with its determined drive for European hegemony.

With the advent of the Daladier government there was a belated rally. The attack on the social legislation of 1936 and the defeat of the strike of 30 November 1938 manifested its intention to restore the authority of the state and with it that of the *patronat*. However, the divisions within the bourgeoisie were by no means resolved and the risks involved in the approaching war intensified them. Still more serious was the fact that the working class, demoralised and defeated as it was, was in no mood to support the foreign policy of a government which was taking away its hard-won 'conquests'. The measures of Daladier and Reynaud may have done something to reassure the bourgeoisie; they did little to prepare the climate of national unity and popular support required for the coming war. The temporary success of the new course was therefore bought at a heavy price; it came too late and it represented the revenge of a class which had felt itself threatened by revolution two years before. If ever a ruling class deserves the judgment 'doomed by history' this was it. Nothing it could do by 1938 could have averted disaster. If it survived the ordeal of defeat and military occupation, as well as the odium of collaboration, this was no tribute to its inner strength or resilience but more a result of external circumstances, of factors over which it had no control.

INDEX OF AUTHORS

Index of Authors

H

Hamon, A., 2
Haupt, G., 37
Huber, M., 58, 59

J

Jaffé, W., 66, 67, 69, 70, 83
Jeanneney, J. M., 115, 127
Jérémac, P., 170
Jèze, G., 46, 49, 58

K

Kalecki, M., 124
Kemp, T., 1, 8, 10, 11, 100
Kriegel, A., 37, 43, 54

L

Landes, D. S., 10, 160, 172
Laufenburger, H., 170
Lefranc, G., 38, 115, 118, 122, 125, 127, 143, 150, 157
Lenin, V. I., 22
Lévy, M., 18
Lévy-Leboyer, M., 10, 16, 17
Lhomme, J., 41
Louis, P., 42

M

Marczewski, J., 10
Marjolin, R., 124, 150
Markovitch, T. J., 171
Mendès-France, P., 115
Mitzman, A., 115, 121
Montet, H., 160

N

Néré, J., 151
Neurisse, A., 73, 77, 126, 154
Nogaro, M. B., 32, 39

O

Ogburn, W. F., 66, 67, 69, 70, 83
Oualid, W., 32, 39, 43

P

Perrot, M., 73, 76, 103, 104
Peschaud, M., 29
Picard, R., 32, 36, 37, 38, 41, 43
Picot, P., 34
Piquenard, C., 32, 39, 43
Poidevin, R., 22

R

Renouvin, P., 29, 33
Reynaud, P., 103
Richardson, H. W., 106
Rist, L., 100
Rostow, W. W., 10
Rueff, J., 82

S

Sauvy, A., 1, 58, 60, 66, 99, 103, 107, 111, 117, 120, 122, 125, 127, 140, 143, 150
Schwob, R., 100
Sée, H., 1
Singer-Kérel, J., 41, 107
Svennilson, I., 87, 106

T

Tiltman, H. H., 99
Trotsky, L., 96, 97
Truchy, H., 46, 47, 48, 49, 50, 58

W

Weil, L., 32, 39
Werth, A., 115
Wright, G., 141, 143

Z

Ziebura, H., 116

INDEX

Index

Index